# Thirteen Cracks

# Thirteen Cracks

## Repairing American Democracy after Trump

Allan J. Lichtman

ROWMAN & LITTLEFIELD
*Lanham • Boulder • New York • London*

Published by Rowman & Littlefield
An imprint of The Rowman & Littlefield Publishing Group, Inc.
4501 Forbes Boulevard, Suite 200, Lanham, Maryland 20706
www.rowman.com

86-90 Paul Street, London EC2A 4NE

Distributed by NATIONAL BOOK NETWORK

British Library Cataloguing in Publication Information Available

**Library of Congress Cataloging-in-Publication Data**

978-1-5381-5651-3 (cloth)
978-1-5381-5652-0 (electronic)

♾™ The paper used in this publication meets the minimum requirements of American National Standard for Information Sciences—Permanence of Paper for Printed Library Materials, ANSI/NISO Z39.48-1992.

# Contents

# Acknowledgments

I would first and foremost like to thank the light of my life, my wife Karyn Strickler. She provided trenchant and insightful commentary on the manuscript. My extraordinary agent Bridget Matzie supported my work throughout the project. Her gentle and persuasive observations made this a much better book. It was a pleasure to work again with my long-time editor Jon Sisk and his excellent staff at Rowman & Littlefield, including Veronica Dove, Susan Hershberg, Deborah Orgel Hudson, Benjamin Knepp, and Elaine McGarraugh. My research assistants, Daniel Ballentyne, Sarah Fahn, Leah Smith, and Andrew Sperling all made important contributions to the book. All errors, of course, I claim for myself.

# Introduction

Democracy is not a state. It is an act, and each generation must do its part to help build what we called the Beloved Community, a nation and world society at peace with itself.

—Democrat U.S. Representative
John Lewis of Georgia, *Final Essay*, 2020

𝒟emocracy is precious. But "everything precious was also vulnerable," wrote the chronicler of culture, Mary H. K. Choi. In the "Golden Age" of democracy following the First World War, the number of functioning democracies soared from just a handful to some twenty-five nations. Then, by 1943, the number fell to only eleven, during a world war that threatened to extinguish democracy where it still prevailed. Democracy rebounded in the late twentieth century but has dwindled again in our own time. A 2020 report by Freedom House, which tracks the status of freedom worldwide, found that democracy has declined or faded away in some twenty-five nations in just the last decade and a half. These once flourishing democracies have descended toward autocracy and are becoming democratic in name only.

We see democracy across the world slipping away before our eyes. The military toppled the government of Myanmar (formerly Burma) and killed hundreds of protesters. Russian President Vladimir Putin imprisoned his main political rival, Alexei Navalny, and extended his right to govern until 2036. Indian Prime Minister Narendra Modi suppressed the free press, peaceful protestors, and the power of judges and parliament. President Alexander Lukashenko of Belarus rigged the

1

most recent presidential election. He detained more than thirty thousand peaceful demonstrators.

Once a global leader in democratic standards, the United States is now at risk of sliding away from democracy unless urgent action is taken soon. "Democracies may die at the hands not of generals, but of elected leaders—presidents or prime ministers who subvert the very processes that brought them to power," warned Steven Levitsky and Daniel Ziblatt in their prescient book, *How Democracies Die*. The *Economist*'s respected Democracy Index for 2020 lists the United States as a "flawed democracy" that ranks only twenty-fifth among nations of the world.

The democratic world looked on aghast when more than 90 percent of Republicans in the U.S. House and Senate refused to impeach or convict Donald Trump for inciting an insurrection and letting rioters run amok in the Capitol. Roland Nelles, the Washington correspondent for Germany's *Der Spiegel*, called the outcome "an unprecedented failure of American democracy." An editorial in the *Sydney Morning Herald* of Australia said that the impeachment failure delivered a "demoralizing blow to the ideals of democracy, justice and accountability." It "will stand for generations as an appalling instance of Republican Party cowardice."

But if you think that American democracy will thrive and endure with the departure of Donald Trump, think again. A will to power drives candidates to seek and win the presidency. It crosses party and ideological lines. The quest for power by presidents has strained the pillars of America's democracy from the early republic to its culmination in the Trump presidency. Trump claimed that he could do whatever he wanted as president. He smashed through the cracks in our democracy more ruthlessly than any predecessor, not excepting Richard Nixon. However, the escapeways remain open for future presidents or even a second coming of Donald Trump after 2024. The loopholes must be closed, and this book offers the essential remedies.

To survive, democracies cannot be static, but need to evolve as societies change and as existing structures fracture or become obsolete. As John Lewis reminded us, democracy "is not a state," but "an act" that requires renewal from every generation of Americans. Vital repair work needs to be accomplished if American democracy is to survive. In James Madison's words, "If men were angels, no government would be necessary. If angels were to govern men, neither external nor internal controls on government would be necessary."

Americans worry about the future of their democracy. A February 2021 survey by Associated Press-National Opinion Research Council (AP-NORC) found that only 16 percent of respondents think democracy in the United States is working "well" or "extremely well." A Pew Research Poll from September 2020 disclosed that just 20 percent of respondents "trust the federal government to do what is right just about always/most of the time." Yet Pew still found that 57 percent of respondents affirmed that, "as Americans, we can always find ways to solve our problems and get what we want."

Fortunately, most Americans still embrace the historic, legal, and customary principles of their democracy. Pew found that "the public places great importance on a broad range of democratic ideals and principles." Overwhelming majorities of respondents agreed that the rights and freedoms of all people should be respected and that elected officials should face serious consequences for misconduct. Americans backed peaceful protests, checks and balances, and an open and transparent government. They agreed that we should acknowledge common facts even if we disagree on politics.

The AP-NORC survey revealed that "more than 8 in 10 Americans think that a fair judiciary, liberties defined by the Constitution, the ability to achieve the 'American Dream,' and a democratically elected government are important for the country's identity." Only 29 percent thought it important to preserve "a culture established by the country's early European immigrants." A Democracy Fund survey from July 2020 found that more than three-quarters of Americans believe that the news media should monitor the president and other politicians. They believe that Congress should exercise oversight of the executive and that Americans should be free to criticize their president.

Yet, the rise of fascism abroad in the 1930s and its reappearance in the world today show that peoples' fears and insecurities can lead to autocracy. What follows is a blueprint for effective, lasting reform that will transcend the administration of any president and restore the public's trust in their government. The good news is that times of crisis typically unleash bursts of structural reform in America's democratic order. "American history actually supports optimism," said the poet known as bell hooks.

After America's troubled presidential transition of power in 1800, the Twelfth Amendment replaced the designation of the vice president as the second-highest vote getter in the Electoral College with the modern president/vice president ticket system. In the aftermath of the Civil War, the Thirteenth Amendment abolished slavery. The Fourteenth established due process rights and equal protection under the law. The Fifteenth prohibited disenfranchisement on account of race, color, or previous condition of servitude. The assassination of President James Garfield in 1881, allegedly by a disgruntled office seeker, led Congress to adopt the first civil service law.

In the early twentieth century, the corruption of democracy by corporate interests prompted adoption of primary elections, personal voter registration, lawmaking by referendum, and the direct election of U.S. senators. The contradiction between fighting for democracy abroad during the First World War and its denial at home led to the enactment of the Nineteenth Amendment on women's suffrage. The savage beatings of civil rights demonstrators in the 1960s produced the Civil Rights Act of 1964 and the Voting Rights Act of 1965.

Following Richard Nixon's Watergate scandal, Congress adopted campaign finance regulations and limitations on presidential prerogatives. It enacted the Ethics in Government Act, which created the office of Independent Counsel to investigate executive misdeeds. The controversial presidential election of 2000 gave rise to the Help America Vote Act of 2002, which improved electoral systems and access to registration. The Great Recession of 2008 led to new controls on corporate abuse. In each of these stressful times, the American people responded with meaningful democratic change.

The remedies proposed here for American democracy are simple, quick, and practical. Most reforms can be implemented through legislation, such as creating a special court to review executive directives. Others require only administrative change, such as authorizing the Department of Justice to name a president as an unindicted coconspirator in a crime. Some require only a private-sector initiative, such as putting in place an instant fact-checking of politicians. "Recovery will be possible only as reinvention of institutions, of what politics means to us, and of what it means to be a democracy, if that is indeed what we choose to be," said Masha Gessen, a scholar of both democracy and autocracy.

As Winston Churchill has reminded us in his own caustic way, democracy is very much worth saving in the pivotal time following the Trump administration. "No one pretends that democracy is perfect or all-wise," he said. "Indeed, it has been said that democracy is the worst form of Government except for all those other forms that have been tried from time to time."

.

# Doing Whatever I Want

## Controlling Autocracy

It would be folly to argue that the people cannot make political mistakes. They can and do make grave mistakes. They know it, they pay the penalty, but compared with the mistakes which have been made by every kind of autocracy they are unimportant.

—U.S. President Calvin Coolidge, 1923

*In a May 19, 1977,* interview with David Frost, Richard Nixon shocked the nation by saying, "When the president does it, that means that it is not illegal." Nixon made this infamous claim more than two and a half years after he resigned the presidency to avoid impeachment and conviction for the Watergate scandals. Incumbent President Jimmy Carter promptly denounced this perversion of a president's authority. He called Nixon's claim a "tragic mistake . . . as past events have shown so dramatically."

Commentators across the land agreed. A *Washington Post* editorial denounced Nixon's "doctrine of gross presidential privilege." *New York Times* reporter James Naughton wrote that "Mr. Nixon unintentionally displayed, more graphically than any critic ever could, the extent to which arrogance, isolation, and mistrust contributed to a warped understanding of his duties and limitations as chief executive." The *Chicago Tribune* editorialized that "the rightful exercise of presidential discretion is not helped by Mr. Nixon's offering the rule that whatever a President [or one of his innumerable deputies] does is legal." *Los Angeles Times* reporter Robert J. Donovan charged that "no simpler formula could be found for changing our system of government, the two-hundredth anniversary of which was celebrated only last July 4."

Thirty-two years later, in a June 2019 interview with ABC News Chief Anchor George Stephanopoulos, Trump made an even more daring claim to presidential authority, not in retirement, but during his incumbency. In response to a question about whether he had tried to fire Special Counsel Robert Mueller, Trump denied the allegation, but added, "Article II [of the U.S. Constitution] allows me to do whatever I want. Article II would have allowed me to fire him." This restatement of French King Louis XIV's infamous assertion that "I am the State," was no Trumpian slip of the tongue. He was not joking, as he often claims to still controversy, and he was not being sarcastic to annoy the media.

A month later, Trump said on the South Lawn of the White House, "Also, take a look at one other thing. It's a thing called Article II. Nobody ever mentions Article II. It gives me all of these rights at a level that nobody has ever seen before." The following week, Trump told a cheering audience of young people at the Turning Point USA Teen Student Action Summit that "I have an Article II, where I have the right to do whatever I want as president." No president in the history of the country, even Nixon, had ever claimed such autocratic sway over America's democracy.

Article II, of course, does not give unlimited power to Nixon, Trump, or any American president. Trump's claim of absolute presidential authority would outrage the nation's founders who devised a Constitution to ensure that no branch of government gains preeminent power. Article II establishes the president as the head of the executive branch of government and the commander-in-chief of the armed forces. It enumerates certain powers such as the granting of pardons. It says that the president "shall take Care that the Laws be faithfully executed," the so-called Take Care clause. These are awesome, but not unlimited powers.

Article I sets guardrails for Article II. It seats within Congress, the first branch of government, all legislative powers, both general and enumerated. As a protection against tyranny, no one branch of government would both make the law and enforce it. Article III further restrains the president by empowering the judiciary to rule on applications of laws and the Constitution. "The powers of government should be so divided and balanced among general bodies of magistracy, as that no one could transcend their legal limits without being effectually checked and restrained by the others," Thomas Jefferson said. "The contest for ages," wrote Senator Daniel Webster a half century later, "has been to rescue liberty from the grasp of executive power."

It is not just Trump. Other presidents have expanded the Take Care clause of Article II to become de facto lawmakers through executive directives (formal executive orders published in the Federal Register and less formal memoranda and proclamations). These directives do not require the approval of Congress, but generally have the force of law.

For better or for worse, presidential directives have changed the course of U.S. history. President Andrew Jackson's second term coincided with a major speculative boom, fueled by soaring land sales in the West, mostly paid for with paper money. Jackson contemplated ways to safeguard "the safety of our currency . . . check the paper system and gambling menace that pervades our land and must if not checked ruin our country and liberty." Without congressional approval, he issued the Specie Circular of 1836, which required purchasers of major tracts of federal land to pay in gold or silver. This directive resulted in a contraction of the currency in 1837 and an economic crisis. Businesses and banks failed, workers lost their jobs, and real estate values crashed.

During the Civil War, President Abraham Lincoln issued his Emancipation Proclamation that liberated slaves in Confederate-controlled territory. The Proclamation at the time freed few slaves, but it turned the war into a crusade to end slavery, not only to save the Union. It liberated millions of slaves when Union forces defeated the Confederate armies. The Proclamation also announced the acceptance of African Americans in the Union Army. Eventually, some two hundred thousand black men enlisted. The Proclamation inspired slavery's opponents, which contributed to final abolition through enactment of the Thirteenth Amendment in 1865.

Set against the historically acclaimed Proclamation is President Lincoln's decision to suspend the constitutional right of habeas corpus, which protects Americans from arbitrary detention without charge. Lincoln believed that disloyal "copperheads" threatened victory on the battlefield and unity at home. Lincoln did not retreat, despite an opinion by the Chief Justice of the U.S. Supreme Court, Roger Taney, sitting as a trial judge, that only Congress could suspend habeas corpus. "Are all the laws but one to go unexecuted," Lincoln said, "and the government itself go to pieces, lest that one be violated?" Through the war's end, his government detained some ten thousand to fifteen thousand persons without a prompt trial.

In 1931, President Herbert Hoover sought to protect an ailing economy by cutting immigration beyond the already diminished levels under the quota law of 1924. The president directed American consuls abroad to deny visas to prospective immigrants who lacked the wealth to support themselves in the United States without becoming a public charge. The directive reduced the flow of immigrants by about 90 percent, a popular result at the time. It did nothing for the economy and blocked many persecuted European Jews from finding refuge in the United States.

To combat the Great Depression and defeat America's enemies in World War II, President Franklin Delano Roosevelt issued 3,721 executive decrees. He more than doubled the output of any other president. With the U.S. financial system on the brink of collapse, FDR declared a "holiday" just after his inauguration on March 4, 1933. By temporarily shuttering the banks and stopping panicked withdrawals, the order kept them solvent until Congress passed reform legislation. A month later, to inject money into the dormant economy, he ordered Americans to exchange their personal holdings of gold for cash. In 1941, to beat Germany in the race for an atomic weapon, FDR established the Office of Scientific Research and Development (OSRD). Its secret S-1 Section, which became the Manhattan Project, developed the world's first atomic bomb.

Like Lincoln, FDR sacrificed the rights of individuals to the demands of war. Japan's surprise attack on Pearl Harbor raised fears of a "yellow peril" that would sabotage the war from within. With support from California's Republican Attorney General Earl Warren, later chief justice of the U.S. Supreme Court, Roosevelt uprooted more than 110,000 West Coast residents of Japanese heritage. Although two-thirds of them were American-born citizens, his administration interned them for the war's duration. In 1988, President Ronald Reagan signed the Civil Liberties Act, which apologized for the internment and authorized reparations for surviving detainees.

In 1948, for the first time in its history, the Democratic Party adopted an ambitious civil rights program. With legislation blocked by southern Democrats in Congress, President Harry Truman acted unilaterally to overturn 170 years of precedent and desegregate the

American armed forces. It was the first time since the Emancipation Proclamation that a president had used his Article II powers to advance minority rights. It was the first major victory for civil rights since Reconstruction. President Lyndon Johnson extended the mandate of the 1964 Civil Rights Act, which prohibited racial or gender discrimination in employment. A 1965 order required federal contractors to take affirmative action to enhance job opportunities for racial minorities. Two years later, an amended order covered women. Affirmative action, its supporters explained, offsets the persistent effects of past discrimination that colorblind policies alone cannot address. Affirmative action programs have expanded employment and educational opportunities for minorities and women, while critics charge it with "reverse discrimination" against white men with allegedly superior qualifications.

President Ronald Reagan's economic program rested on tax cuts and deregulation. He deregulated business, not only to spur competition, but also to reduce the costs of health, safety, energy, environmental, and civil rights regulations. The number of pages in the federal register, a rough gauge of regulation, fell by a third during Reagan's first two years after rising by more than 50 percent under President Carter. Reagan achieved that goal largely by executive decree. A month into his first term, Reagan *required* regulatory agencies to conduct cost/benefit analyses of regulations and submit them to the Office of Management and Budget for review.

Among its post-Watergate reforms, Congress empowered the federal government to take custody of records from the administrations of former presidents and provide the public access within twelve years. In 2001, President George W. Bush gutted this reform. The president unilaterally restricted access to presidential records "reflecting military, diplomatic, or national security secrets, Presidential communications, legal advice, legal work, or the deliberative processes of the President and the President's advisers." He essentially covered every notable presidential record. President Barack Obama revoked Bush's order upon taking office in 2009.

Several presidents have established significant new federal agencies and programs through executive orders. In May 1935, with unemployment in double digits, Roosevelt launched a federal employment program, the Works Progress Administration (WPA). Between 1935 and its termination in 1943, the WPA employed 8.5 million workers. In 1961, President John F. Kennedy established the Peace Corps. He believed that by helping those "struggling to break the bonds of mass misery" in "the huts and villages of half the globe," Corps volunteers would dispel the "Ugly American" image and counter Soviet influence in the less-developed world. From 1961 to 2020, 235,000 Americans served in the Peace Corps. The federal government's piecemeal response to natural and man-made disasters prompted President Jimmy Carter to create the Federal Emergency Management Administration (FEMA) in 1979. With a workforce of twenty thousand, FEMA is now part of the Department of Homeland Security. Frustrated by Congress's failure to enact comprehensive immigration reform, President Obama established in 2012 the Deferred Action for Childhood Arrival program (DACA). It provides some seven hundred thousand undocumented immigrants, who came to the United States as children, protection from deportation and eligibility for work permits in the United States.

Although the courts have given broad latitude for executive directives, they have imposed limitations on Article II powers. In 1952, the U.S. Supreme Court ruled against the seizure of steel plants by President Truman during the Korean War. The majority opinion found that President Truman's "order does not direct that a congressional policy be executed in a manner prescribed by Congress—it directs that a presidential policy be executed in a manner prescribed by the President." In his concurring opinion, Justice Robert Jackson explained that first, presidential authority was at its highest "pursuant to an express or implied authorization of Congress." Second, and more limited, are directives when Congress has been silent on an issue. Third, presidential "power is at its lowest ebb," when the president "takes measures incompatible with the expressed or implied will of Congress." Thus, the president has minimal Article II authority when attempting to act contrary to the intent of Congress. Simply put, the Take Care clause in Article II does not authorize a president to do whatever he wants.

President Trump has abused his Article II authority to become a prolific one-man lawmaker and enforcement officer, notably when it comes to controversial immigration policy. Professor Michele Waslin of George Mason University found that presidents from Harry Truman to Barack Obama had collectively issued twelve total substantive policy directives on immigration. Truman issued half of these directives during the refugee crisis after World War II. By October 2019, President Trump had issued fifteen such directives. He later issued several more, far exceeding the total of policy decrees on immigration by all prior presidents combined since the Second World War.

In many cases, federal courts have reined in Trump's Article II overreach and invalidated his orders for violating federal law and the Constitution. Yet, other directives have set a dangerous precedent for future autocratically inclined presidents. On the weeklong anniversary of his inauguration, Trump partly fulfilled a campaign pledge when by executive order he blocked, for ninety days, immigration from seven predominantly Muslim nations. He prohibited refugees from entering America for 120 days and suspended indefinitely the admission of refugees from Syria.

Trump became the first president to breach the letter and intent of the Immigration Act of 1965. The act rejected quotas of national origin dating from the xenophobic 1920s, and opened immigration equally to people across the world. President Lyndon Johnson said at the signing ceremony that by ending quotas, the act "corrects a cruel and enduring wrong in the conduct of the American nation." It "will really make us truer to ourselves both as a country and as a people." Until Trump, every subsequent American president has avowed similar ideals.

The Ninth Circuit Court of Appeals rejected Trump's contention that he had the power to exempt immigration policy from judicial review. It ruled that "there is no precedent to support this claimed un-reviewability, which runs contrary to the fundamental structure of our constitutional democracy." It said, "Neither the Supreme Court nor our court has ever held that courts lack the authority to review executive action in those arenas for compliance with the Constitution." Trump finally secured approval for a third, diluted travel ban in a 5 to 4 decision by the U.S. Supreme Court. The Court agreed that a review of the revised ban fell within its jurisdiction but found that it did not violate the law or the Constitution.

Trump revoked President Obama's protection of some seven hundred thousand DREAMers through his DACA program and the protection of more than three hundred thousand migrants from the dangerous countries of El Salvador, Honduras, and Haiti under the Temporary Protective Status program. He introduced a ban on asylum to migrants at America's southern border unless they already had been denied asylum in Mexico or other countries of passage. He denied some federal grants to so-called sanctuary jurisdictions that did not cooperate with the enforcement of federal immigration laws. Trump ruled that federal officials could deny green cards (legal residence) to claimants who might participate in federal benefit programs such as Food Stamps and Medicaid. He used his executive powers to divert billions of dollars in military appropriations to build a wall at the Mexican border.

In his most reviled decision, Trump separated migrant families and detained children. A report by the Inspector General (IG) for the U.S. Department of Justice issued on January 14, 2021, found that the Trump administration had "ordered a change in long-standing federal practice." In just a few months, "from April to June 2018, more than 3,000 children were separated from their families." There was a lack of coordination and planning for "the zero-tolerance policy," and children suffered from deplorable conditions in detention facilities. Through December 2020, the administration had not located the parents of 628 migrant children.

In April 2020, Trump used public distraction during the CO-VID-19 pandemic to impose a 60-day moratorium on the issuance of green cards to most immigrants. In June 2020, he extended that freeze and suspended H-1B visas for skilled foreign workers until the end of 2020. Trump prohibited any new international students from entering the United States for online-only instruction. He made it harder for legal immigrants to become U.S. citizens, and likely Democratic voters, by making the citizenship test more difficult and nearly doubling the cost of naturalization from $640 to $1,160. Trump issued an executive memorandum to exclude undocumented immigrants from the census count that apportions congressional districts and Electoral College votes among the states. This change would have reduced representation in heavily Hispanic states and skewed the allocation of nearly a trillion dollars in census-based federal aid to communities in need.

Although the legal process usually grinds on for years, many federal tribunals from district courts to the Supreme Court have invalidated Trump's expansion of his Article II authority over immigration policy. These adverse decisions exceeded negative rulings on all substantive executive orders on all matters by previous presidents from Truman to Obama.

For example, the Supreme Court ruled that Trump's attempt to dismantle DACA was an "arbitrary and capricious" extension of executive authority that violated the Administrative Procedure Act's mandate for "a reasoned explanation," Judge Eric D. Miller, a Trump appointee, concurred in the Ninth Circuit Court's ruling against Trump's order denying asylum to pass-through migrants. He found Trump's "deficient" justification "particularly troubling because the rule represents such a major change to policy—perhaps the most significant change to American asylum in a generation." Federal District Court Judge Edward M. Chen found that Trump's order terminating the Temporary Protected Status program "may have been done in order to implement and justify a pre-ordained result desired by the White House . . . based on animus against non-white, non-European immigrants in violation of Equal Protection guaranteed by the Constitution." Federal District Court Judge Dana Sabraw ruled that the president's policies of family separation and child detention "belie measured and ordered governance, which is central to the concept of due process enshrined in our Constitution."

During the Obama years, Republicans had condemned the alleged abuse of the president's Article II powers, despite their applause under Trump. In 2014, the Republican majority in the U.S. House authorized House Speaker John Boehner to sue Obama for modifying the Affordable Care Act by executive order. "Only the Legislative Branch has the power to legislate," Boehner said. "The current president believes he has the power to make his own laws—at times even boasting about it." However, "the House has an obligation to stand up for the Legislative Branch, and the Constitution, and that is exactly what we will do." After several months of delay, Boehner filed the lawsuit, one of many court challenges to Obamacare that have so far failed to shred the program.

In 2015, 113 House Republicans backed a lawsuit by Republican state attorneys general to overturn Obama's directive on DACA. His order "changes the law and sets a new policy," they charged, "exceeding the executive's constitutional authority and disrupting the delicate balance of powers." Republican Bob Goodlatte, chair of the House Judiciary Committee, added, "President Obama's decision to ignore the limits placed on his power and act unilaterally to rewrite our nation's immigration laws are an affront to the Constitution."

Donald Trump and Mike Pence joined this testy chorus of fellow Republicans. Obama could not negotiate a deal with Congress and "now he has to use executive action," Trump said, "and this is a very, very dangerous thing." He added that "we're looking now at a situation that should absolutely not pass muster in terms of constitutionality," and Obama "certainly could be impeached" for his overreach. Pence said, "I think it would be a profound mistake for the president of the United States to overturn American immigration law with the stroke of a pen. Issues of this magnitude should always be resolved with the consent of the American people."

The strength of executive directives is that they do not require authorization from Congress. Their weakness is that a succeeding president can revoke them on his own authority. When President Joe Biden wiped out many of Trump's executive decrees, Republicans rediscovered their aversion to executive action. Republican Senator Joni Ernst of Iowa said that Biden "is not just breaking norms, he is obliterating them." Republican Senator John Barrasso from Wyoming said, "we see the Biden administration adopting a flawed substitute, as they say, for legislation. . . . They didn't send us here to stand by and watch a President go with one executive order after another." Senate Republican leader Mitch McConnell slammed Biden's use of executive orders as inconsistent with his pledge to be a consensus leader. "In one week," McConnell complained, "he signed more than thirty unilateral actions."

Presidential directives are powerful tools under Article II that can do much good but are also susceptible to misuse. President George Washington forcefully exercised his powers under Article II, but within legal limits. "It is my duty to see the Laws executed," he said, "to permit them to be trampled upon with impunity would be repugnant to it."

## THE FIX: ESTABLISH A
## COURT OF PRESIDENTIAL DIRECTIVES

Control over presidential overreach should not depend on partisan politics or on endless litigation. Congress should check a president's abuse of Article II powers through a federal court of special jurisdiction—the Court of Presidential Directives. It would resolve quickly and expertly litigation challenging presidential directives. This is not a radical idea. Existing courts of special jurisdiction include the Court of Federal Claims, the Court of International Trade, the Court of Appeals for Veterans Claims, the Tax Court, and the Foreign Intelligence Surveillance Court. These tribunals deal only with designated types of cases and have their own budgets and rules in place to expedite review. Judges of special courts are typically appointed for fixed terms and focus on just one aspect of the law and the Constitution.

But couldn't a Trump 2.0 simply stack such a court with loyalists? The Constitution already prevents this. Congress could entrust appointments to the U.S. Supreme Court, not to the president, or even Congress. The Constitution's Appointments Clause includes the little-known provision that "the Congress may by Law vest the Appointment of such inferior Officers, as they think proper, in the President alone, in the Courts of Law, or in the Heads of Departments." In *Freytag v. Commissioner*, the U.S. Supreme Court ruled in 1991 that the chief justice of the tax court could appoint special tax court judges who were "inferior officers" under the Constitution and subject to judicial appointment because they "exercise significant discretion."

In establishing a new special court, Congress can provide safeguards for ideological balance. It could require the Supreme Court to select an equal number of judges from a list submitted by the president and the Senate leader of the opposition party. Vacancies would be filled from this same list. Some states already follow this process for judicial appointments and Congress has adopted similar rules for ideological balance in the legislation that established the Federal Election Commission. For this court, Justice Jackson's tripartite test from the steel plant seizure case would balance the legitimate exercise of Article II power against its abuses.

# Congress Be Damned

## *Restoring Accountability*

> As a member of Congress, a coequal branch of government, designed by our founders to provide checks and balances on the executive branch, I believe that lawmakers must fulfill our oversight duty.
>
> —Republican U.S. Representative
> Will Hurd of Texas, 2018

$\mathscr{A}$s spring slid into the sweltering heat of a Washington, D.C., summer, controversy about bribery and extortion swirled around the White House. The opposition party that controlled the U.S. House of Representatives began investigating the president's alleged abuses of power as a prelude to impeachment. The president refused to cooperate. He accused Congress of overstepping its authority to interrogate an independent branch of government. He called the investigation a partisan vendetta and claimed that the chair of the investigating committee harbored a personal grudge against him. The year was 1860; the president was Democrat James Buchanan.

Buchanan resisted the committee's every attempt to question administration witnesses or acquire documents. "I solemnly protest against these proceedings of the House of Representatives," Buchanan wrote. "They are in violation of the rights of the coordinate executive branch of the Government, and subversive of its constitutional independence; because they are calculated to foster a band of interested parasites and informers" intent upon "furnishing material for harassing him, degrading him in the eyes of the country." He warned of "a reign of terror" if a president submitted to "this terrible secret inquisitorial power" of the House.

The committee's report decried President Buchanan for "protect[ing] those who might choose to disobey the summons of the Speaker of the House, or who, having obeyed the summons, might refuse to testify before your committee." Still, it conducted the investigation "to as great an extent as the time and means allowed." Obstructing Democrats denounced the committee's closed-door sessions as "Star Chamber proceedings." Although the committee did not recommend impeachment, it uncovered abuses of power. Today, Buchanan is one of the least esteemed presidents.

No subsequent president, including Richard Nixon, has so stubbornly asserted his right to override congressional oversight—until Donald Trump. Federal District Court Judge Amit P. Mehta observed, "Some 160 years later, President Donald J. Trump has taken up the fight" of James Buchanan. Trump's defiance of Congress is yet more categorical and sweeping than Buchanan's. He has arrogated to himself control over the legitimacy of any congressional inquiry, even on impeachment, when the powers of Congress are at their height.

A president's defiance of congressional oversight threatens the checks and balances that protect our democracy from tyranny. America's Framers understood that investigations by Congress, the branch of government closest to the people, monitored the conduct of a powerful executive. Otherwise, without fear of retribution, a president could place his own interests ahead of those of the American people. Delegate George Mason of Virginia said at the Constitutional Convention of 1787 that members of Congress "are not only Legislators but they possess inquisitorial powers. They must meet frequently to inspect the Conduct of the public offices."

James Madison of Virginia, the father of the Constitution, wrote that "in republican government, the legislative authority necessarily predominates." It "alone has access to the pockets of the people," enabling it to extend "the sphere of its activity" and draw "all power into its impetuous vortex." He said that "in framing a government, which is to be administered by men over men, the great difficulty is this: You must first enable the government to control the governed; and in the next place, oblige it to control itself."

More than a century later, another president, the scholarly Woodrow Wilson, explained:

It is the proper duty of a representative body to look diligently into every affair of government and to talk much about what it sees. It is meant to be the eyes and the voice, and to embody the wisdom and will of its constituents. Unless Congress have and use every means of acquainting itself with the acts and the disposition of the administrative agents of the government, the country must be helpless to learn how it is being served.

The U.S. Supreme Court agreed with Wilson. A 1975 majority opinion by Chief Justice Warren Burger, emphasized that "this Court has often noted that the power to investigate is inherent in the power to make laws." Further, the "issuance of subpoenas such as the one in question here has long been held to be a legitimate use by Congress of its power to investigate."

Investigations ground Congress's power of impeachment, which is democracy's ultimate weapon against a rogue executive. Alexander Hamilton said that impeachment will "proceed from the misconduct of public men, or in other words, from the abuse or violation of some public trust." He recognized that politics cannot be scrubbed out of an impeachment process that the Framers placed in an elected body, not in the judiciary. He said that impeachments "are of a nature which may with peculiar propriety be denominated POLITICAL as they relate chiefly to injuries done immediately to society itself."

Congressional investigations of the executive began in the first U.S. Congress that convened in 1789. The House of Representatives organized a select committee to probe the handling of government finances. Madison said that the "House should possess itself of the fullest information in order to do justice to the country and to public officers." The second Congress investigated how Native American warriors at the Battle of the Wabash defeated the army of U.S. General Arthur St. Clair. The House called "for such persons, papers, and records, as may be necessary to assist their inquiries." It negotiated with Commander-in-Chief Washington to set the terms and conditions for disclosure.

Although Congress's probe of St. Clair's defeat could embarrass the president, Washington supported the investigation of his chosen general and encouraged his testimony. "As the House of Representatives have been pleased to institute an enquiry into the causes of the failure of the late expedition," Washington wrote to St. Clair, "I should hope an opportunity would thereby be afforded you, of explaining your conduct, in a manner satisfactory to the public and yourself." Washington directed his secretary of war, Henry Knox, to provide all the requested documents.

Balanced against the oversight powers of Congress is the doctrine of executive privilege, which protects from congressional scrutiny certain confidential communications within the executive branch. Dwight Eisenhower in 1954 became the first president to use the term executive privilege, but the practice began under President Washington. Although Washington typically cooperated with congressional investigators, he did not do so universally. The president declined to submit to the House of Representatives negotiating documents for the 1794 Jay Treaty with Britain. Washington reasoned that "the nature of foreign negotiations requires caution, and their success must often depend on secrecy." He said that "the power of making treaties" was limited to "the President, with the advice and consent of the Senate," thus "confining it to a small number of members." The House, he said, had no role in the treaty process. Giving it access to sensitive material, "would be to establish a dangerous precedent." Thus was born the doctrine of executive privilege.

Washington recognized limitations on the privilege. He had shared negotiating documents on the treaty with the Senate. He acknowledged that he would provide sensitive documents to the House, when it had legitimate reasons for access, at least pursuant to an impeachment inquiry. "It does not occur that the inspection of the papers asked for can be relative to any purpose under the cognizance of the House of Representatives," Washington wrote, "except that of an impeachment, which the resolution [passed by the House for access] has not expressed."

The federal courts have recognized the doctrine of executive privilege but limited its application. The privilege is at its height for core communications, oral or documentary, on presidential decision making by close advisers. This is the "presidential communications privilege." The privilege is weakest when applied to other communications by executive branch officials. This is the "deliberative process privilege." Congress can override either privilege when information is essential to its oversight or legislative functions and cannot be obtained by other means.

Although no president before Donald Trump, including James Buchanan, has claimed absolute immunity from any congressional oversight, clashes between Congress and presidents are endemic to American democracy. They transcend party lines and are not dependent on the character and personalities of the antagonists. The clashes reflect a built-in tension between Congress's right to know and presidents' will to power.

In the 1830s, opposition leaders reviled President Andrew Jackson as a dictator—"King Andrew the First"—and a demagogue. In 1834, an anti-Jackson majority in the U.S. Senate demanded that the president turn over an internal memo about his removal of federal deposits from the Bank of the United States. Jackson had hoped to kill the bank, which he believed protected the wealthy elites that he had pledged to drive out of power. When Jackson refused, for the first and only time the Senate voted to censure a president. The censure resolution declared that Jackson had "assumed upon himself authority and power not conferred by the Constitution and law, but in derogation of both."

When Democrats regained the Senate majority in 1837, they revoked the censure. The Secretary of the Senate drew heavy black lines around the censorship resolution and boldly proclaimed, "Expunged by of the Senate." The opposition leader, Whig Senator Henry Clay, who had lost to Jackson in the presidential election of 1832, dressed in black to mourn the death of the Republic. He told the Senate "that henceforward, no matter what daring or outrageous act any president may perform, you have forever hermetically sealed the mouth of the Senate."

In late January 1837, Jackson's adversaries took a parting shot at the lame duck president. Under the leadership of anti-Jackson, Whig Representative Henry A. Wise, a Select Committee of the House of Representatives began investigating corruption and abuse in federal departments and agencies. The committee issued a wide-ranging request for administration documents and testimony. President Jackson rejected this request. He complained that the committee did not ask officials to explain "any particular transaction." Instead, "you request myself and the heads of the departments to become our own accusers, and to furnish the evidence to convict ourselves." He pledged to "repel" such requests "as an invasion of the principles of justice, as well as the Constitution; and I shall esteem it my sacred duty to the people of the United States, to resist them as I would the establishment of a Spanish inquisition."

Wise responded that Jackson "assumes to control as well as to supervise the proceedings of the House." If Congress could not "inquire into the official conduct of an administration," federal officials "would, in effect, become irresponsible" judges of their own acts. Without inquiry the House could not carry out its constitutional functions to legislate or impeach a dangerous president. Executive officers, he insisted, "belong to the *people*," but "without strict superintendence over them by the people or by their representatives, the people soon belong to *them*." The dispute remained in limbo since Jackson's term quickly expired on March 4, 1837.

In 1948, the Republican-led House Un-American Activities Committee subpoenaed the Truman administration to release information from an FBI file on the Director of the National Bureau of Standards, Dr. Edward Condon. Committee members suspected Condon of disloyalty. President Truman rejected the demand. He ordered the heads of executive agencies to spurn all subpoenas for confidential loyalty information that could compromise national security and violate individual rights. Truman held firm, even after the full House voted 300 to 29 directing him to release the information on Condon.

A fiery young committee member from California named Richard Nixon charged the president with "willfully obstructing an investigation which is absolutely essential to the security of each and every person in this country." He called upon Truman to release all relevant information on communist infiltration of the federal government. Truman responded that his own stringent internal loyalty program had scrubbed the government clean of subversion. He claimed that Republicans "have attempted to usurp the functions of the federal grand juries and of the courts" and "trampled on the individual freedoms which distinguish American ideals from totalitarian doctrine." The dispute became moot when the president won reelection in 1948 and his Democrats regained control over both houses of Congress.

In 1982, a House Subcommittee investigated charges that the Environmental Protection Agency had politically manipulated its implementation of the Superfund program for the treatment of hazardous waste sites. In response to a subpoena for records on cleanup programs, President Ronald Reagan instructed the EPA administrator Anne M. Gorsuch (the mother of U.S. Supreme Court Justice Neil Gorsuch) to claim executive privilege and withhold the information. On December

16, a bipartisan majority of the House of Representatives cited Gorsuch for contempt of Congress. Although Gorsuch lacked cabinet status, she became the first head of a federal agency that Congress held in contempt.

Just moments after the contempt vote, the Justice Department sued the House. In February 1983, Federal District Court Judge John Lewis Smith Jr. dismissed the case on procedural grounds. He did not rule on the assertion of executive privilege but encouraged "the two branches to settle their differences without further judicial involvement. Compromise and cooperation, rather than confrontation, should be the aim of the parties." Gorsuch resigned a month later, and the parties reached a compromise on submission of the documents.

In 2010 and 2011, federal agents conducted a sting operation called Fast and Furious. They allowed illegal purchases of firearms to take place, for the purpose of tracing the guns to cartel traffickers and placing them under arrest. However, agents lost track of more than half of some two thousand supposedly tagged guns, some of which turned up at murder scenes. The U.S. House Oversight Committee, under the control of Republicans, subpoenaed Fast and Furious documents. President Barack Obama then asserted executive privilege to allow Attorney General Eric Holder to withhold some confidential records. That was the only time Obama claimed executive privilege under his watch. On June 28, 2012, the full House voted largely along party lines to hold the attorney general in contempt of Congress for failing to provide subpoenaed documents. This was the first time in U.S. history that Congress had cited an incumbent cabinet member for contempt. After protracted litigation, the parties finally settled the matter in April 2019, more than two years after Obama left office.

Trump's impactful clashes with Congress began when the April 2019 report of Special Counsel Robert Mueller revealed that Trump had ordered White House Counsel Don McGahn to fire Mueller. When McGahn refused, Trump ordered him to lie and write a denial letter for the record. Democrats in the U.S. House of Representatives subpoenaed McGahn to testify and to produce relevant documents, pursuant to their review of a possible impeachment for obstruction of justice. The president called the subpoena "ridiculous," and claimed immunity from further inquiry. "I'd say it's enough," the president declared. "We are fighting all the subpoenas."

President Trump did not claim to have discussed sensitive issues with McGahn that could jeopardize U.S. security or other compelling national interests. For Trump, nothing coming from the Democratic-controlled U.S. House qualified as legitimate oversight. "These aren't, like, impartial people. The Democrats are trying to win 2020," Trump said. "The only way they can luck out is by constantly going after me on nonsense."

During oral argument in the McGahn case before a panel of the D.C. Court of Appeals, Judge Thomas Griffith, an appointee of President George W. Bush, asked, "Has there ever been an instance of such broad-scale defiance of congressional requests for information in the history of the Republic?" After a pause, in a moment of candor, the Department of Justice's lawyer responded, "Not to my knowledge." He then added his unfounded belief that "the President would say, 'never before has Congress engaged in the sort of illegitimate things they're doing.'" The case dragged on until McGahn reached an agreement with the Biden administration to testify before Congress.

Trump again defied congressional oversight during the 2019 impeachment process. The full House ratified two articles of impeachment on December 18, 2019. The first article charged the president with abuse of power for pressuring Ukrainian president Volodymyr Zelensky to announce politically beneficial investigations. The second article charged him with obstruction of Congress. Once the inquiry began, the president attempted to block congressional access to all witnesses and documents. Trump released a reconstruction of the call with Zelensky, which he called "perfect." He claimed that it exonerated him of wrongdoing. Democrats in Congress and most Americans thought otherwise. The publication of the call log was the first and the last bit of notable information that the Trump administration provided Congress.

Although the Constitution grants the House "sole Power of Impeachment," White House Counsel Pat Cipollone argued that the president had authority to judge the legitimacy of an impeachment inquiry. Like President Buchanan, he claimed that the House's inquiry was "constitutionally invalid," and that "President Trump and his Administration cannot participate in your partisan and unconstitutional inquiry." Trump's lawyers argued that the House should have petitioned the courts to enforce its subpoenas. They knew full well that the interminable judicial process would likely drag on through the 2020 presidential election. Like the characters from Joseph Heller's novel on Second World War Air Force fighters, Trump's lawyers put congressional investigators into a catch-22 no-win trap. The lawyers claimed in other litigation that courts cannot enforce congressional subpoenas. The only remedy for a recalcitrant president, they said, was impeachment, which they were simultaneously obstructing. "Catch-22 says they have a right to do anything we can't stop them from doing," said a trapped airman in Heller's book.

Trump's impeachment defense ultimately hinged on the extreme claim that a president could do whatever might advance his reelection prospects short of committing a serious, indictable crime. The president's handpicked constitutional expert, Alan Dershowitz, testified on the Senate floor that "every public official that I know believes that his election is in the public interest. . . . If a president does something which he believes will help him get elected in the public interest, that cannot be the kind of quid pro quo that results in impeachment."

This pernicious doctrine, which Dershowitz failed to corroborate with judicial or scholarly authority, represented what the founders feared most about a runaway president. Framer Gouverneur Morris said, "The Executive ought, therefore, to be impeachable for treachery" and "corrupting his Electors." Dershowitz's criterion would immunize a president from impeachment if, for example, prior to an election he convinced state legislatures controlled by his party into disregarding the popular vote in their states and guaranteeing him their slate of electors.

Another major dispute between the president and Congress arose in 2019, when congressional committees voted to subpoena President Trump's tax records. Trump's protracted litigation over the subpoena led to a 7-2 U.S. Supreme Court decision released on July 9, 2020, the last day of the term. The majority opinion by Chief Justice John Roberts said that, historically, "Disputes over congressional demands for presidential documents have been resolved by the political branches through negotiation and compromise without involving this Court. The Court recognizes that this dispute is the first of its kind to reach the Court." No prior president, including the discredited Buchanan, had categorically refused to negotiate with Congress and assert the right to decide unilaterally the legitimacy of all congressional subpoenas.

"(W)e cannot conclude that absolute immunity is necessary or appropriate under Article II or the Supremacy Clause. Our dissenting colleagues agree," Roberts wrote. "Each House has power 'to secure needed information' in order to legislate," he added. The Court rejected Trump's claim of a right to reject subpoenas unilaterally "without recognizing distinctions between privileged and nonprivileged information," or "Congress's important interests in conducting inquiries to obtain the information it needs to legislate effectively."

Roberts rejected absolute immunity in favor of a balanced approach that remanded the case to a lower court under a four-part test, largely consistent with precedent. First, how compelling is the legislative purpose? Second, is the subpoena narrowly tailored "to support Congress's legislative objective?" Third, what evidence had Congress presented to "establish that a subpoena advances a valid legislative purpose." Fourth, what are "the burdens imposed on the President by a subpoena."

Attorney General William Barr admitted that Trump had lost on his immunity claims. He said, "We are disappointed in the decision to the extent that it did not accept our argument, the government's argument about the extent of the president's immunity." Trump raged that he was the victim of "a political witch hunt" and a "hoax," even though both of his Supreme Court appointees, Neil Gorsuch and Brett Kavanaugh, had joined the majority opinion. "In our system of government, as this court has often stated, no one is above the law. That principle applies, of course, to a president," Kavanaugh wrote in a concurring opinion. Trump had no intention of cooperating with Congress and continued to fight the subpoenas, losing in both the district and appellate courts. As of April 2021, the matter remained pending in the Court.

With litigation unresolved through the 2020 elections, Trump won politically, no matter the final legal outcome, as if concealing of information from Congress and the American people was a cause for rejoicing. Even if Trump's litigation did not last for generations as in Charles Dickens's imaginary case of *Jarndyce v. Jarndyce*, it lingered in the courts long enough for the issue to lose political steam. This is how Trump exploits a loophole in our political system to override the powers of Congress to police a president. He blatantly disregards the rules, and before the courts and due process can force him to comply, the matter has passed—it is too late. Here is where the real problem lies. Even if courts quash presidential attempts at blocking oversight, Trump's style of resistance does create endless delays.

With the party balance between the president and Congress shifting over time, efforts to strengthen the supervisory powers of Congress should not be a partisan project. Both Democrats and Republicans have worried about the presidential resistance to congressional authority. "[T]he legislative branch established in Article I remains the most closely connected to the views of our nation's citizens to this day. The importance of that role and responsibility cannot be overstated," said conservative Republican Representative Tom Cole of Oklahoma. "Though the shift has been gradual, I have long been concerned by Congress ceding some of its authority as well as presidents of both parties claiming power that belongs to the legislative branch."

## THE FIX: FLEXING CONGRESSIONAL MUSCLE

We must begin repairing the executive's obstruction of Congress by punishing officials where it hurts: in their pocketbooks. The president and vice president and department and agency heads have discretionary funds. When those officials defy subpoenas, Congress should unleash its power of the purse to slash their discretionary budgets. In James Madison's words, the power of the purse "may, in fact, be regarded as the most complete and effectual weapon with which the Constitution can arm the immediate representatives of the people, for obtaining a redress of every grievance, and for carrying into effect every just and salutary measure."

For example, in 1908, Congress prohibited any spending on the Marine Corps unless President Theodore Roosevelt revoked his decree to station marines only on shore and not aboard naval vessels. In 1971, Congress effectively cut off the war in Cambodia with the Cooper-Church Amendment that banned the use of any funds for ground troops or advisors in that country. In 1984, the Boland Amendment prohibited federal agencies, directly or indirectly, from using funds for military or paramilitary operations in Nicaragua. Attempts by Reagan administration officials to circumvent this amendment led to the Iran/Contra scandal that nearly toppled Reagan's presidency. In 1993, the Byrd Amendment set financial conditions on military intervention in Somalia. Since 1986, Congress has enacted fiscal measures that restricted U.S. aid to countries where a military coup overthrew a democratically elected government.

The Senate can retaliate against a recalcitrant president through its power to approve presidential appointments. Senators may hold up appointments, both to punish and deter presidential obstruction of congressional authority. While the president may fill vacancies in the executive branch with acting officials at least for a time, lifetime judicial appointments require Senate approval.

Congress should strengthen its logistical support by increasing the meager budgets for the Government Accountability Office, the Congressional Budget Office, and the Congressional Research Service. It needs to raise employees' salaries and streamline outdated hiring practices to attract and retain the best analysts. It should adopt its own version of the Justice Department's Office of Legal Counsel (OLC), to provide expert opinion on legal matters.

Finally, Congress may—as a last resort in extreme cases—awaken its inherent contempt, by punishing obstruction without recourse to prosecution by the Department of Justice. Under this power Congress, like a judge, could fine or even jail persons that it found in contempt for resisting lawful subpoenas. While Congress has neglected inherent contempt in modern times, the U.S Supreme Court has upheld its legitimacy. In the 1920s, a Senate select committee in the context of its inquiry into anti-corruption laws, subpoenaed Mally S. Daugherty, the brother of the shady former U.S. Attorney General Harry M. Daugherty. When Daugherty refused to comply, the Senate issued a warrant for his detention. John J. McGrain, a sergeant at arms for the Senate, took Daugherty into custody. The U.S. Supreme Court rejected Daugherty's petition to nullify his arrest and upheld Congress's arrest power under inherent contempt. "We are of opinion that the power of inquiry—with process to enforce it—is an essential and appropriate auxiliary to the legislative function," the Court said. It noted presciently that "experience has taught that mere requests for such information often are unavailing . . . so some means of compulsion are essential to obtain what is needed." The Court concluded that "the investigation was ordered for a legitimate object; that the witness wrongfully refused to appear and testify before the committee and was lawfully attached."

## • 3 •

# Russia Is Listening

## *Defending America's Sovereignty*

President Putin and the Russian security services . . . weaponize our own political opposition research and false narratives. When we are consumed by partisan rancor, we cannot combat these external forces as they seek to divide us against each other, degrade our institutions, and destroy the faith of the American people in our democracy.

—Former Trump Administration Advisor for
Europe and Russia Fiona Hill, 2019

𝒯he people of France, inspired by the American Revolution, rebelled against their king in 1789 and raised up the first major republic on European soil since antiquity. The fledgling republic endured invasions from European kings fearful of the French precedent. In 1793, France dispatched Edmond-Charles Genet as ambassador to the United States. He styled himself "Citizen Genet" after the republic's egalitarian ideal.

Genet, who recognized no international boundaries, meddled in American politics. With France at war with Britain, Genet held public events on behalf of France. He encouraged U.S. citizens to violate the proclamation of neutrality that President George Washington had issued in April 1793. Genet even commissioned privateers to intercept British shipping. During public meetings, citizens denounced Genet's meddling as "an infringement of the Sovereignty of the people" and "a daring insult to the people of America." An exasperated Washington, equally concerned about the preservation of American sovereignty, demanded Genet's return to France. By then, the French government had changed hands and repudiated Genet, who could not safely return home. He eventually gained asylum in the United States.

31

In 1898, another ambassador, Spain's envoy to the United States, Enrique Dupuy de Lôme, meddled in American affairs. He wrote a letter critical of President William McKinley to a friend in Cuba, which was embroiled in a revolt against Spanish rule. The ambassador, who feared that the United States would intervene in support of Cuban rebels, wrote that "besides the natural and inevitable coarseness with which he repeats all that the press and public opinion of Spain has said of Weyler [Spain's governor-general of Cuba], it shows once more that McKinley is weak and catering to the rabble, and, besides, a low politician, who desires to leave a door open to me and to stand well with the jingoes of his party."

When this letter turned up in the press, President McKinley demanded an apology and forced de Lôme to resign. The ambassador insisted to deaf ears that the letter expressed only his personal views. Public outrage over the de Lôme fiasco figured in McKinley's decision to wage war against Spain and seek to liberate Cuba.

For America's Framers, foreign interference posed the gravest threat to their democratic republic. Hamilton noted that "foreign influence is the Grecian horse to a republic." He said, "These most deadly adversaries of republican government might naturally have been expected to make their approaches from more than one quarter, but chiefly from the desire in foreign powers to gain an improper ascendant in our councils. How could they better gratify this, than by raising a creature of their own to the chief magistracy of the Union?" George Washington wrote that "against the insidious wiles of foreign influence . . . the jealousy of a free people ought to be constantly awake, since history and experience prove that foreign influence is one of the most baneful foes of republican government."

Foreign adversaries, the Framers worried, might subvert America's democratic elections. "Foreign powers" would seize "the opportunity to mix their intrigues & influence with the election," warned James Madison. In a 2012 decision, the U.S. Supreme Court reaffirmed what America's founders understood so well, that "fundamental to the definition of our national political community" is that "foreign citizens do not have a constitutional right to participate in, and thus may be excluded from, activities of democratic self-government."

Conservatives have forcefully defended America's sovereignty against foreign influence, even by opposing international organizations and agreements. Conservatives in the U.S. Senate voted against America's participation in the League of Nations in 1919 and later rejected the Convention on the Rights of Persons with Disabilities, the Arms Trade Treaty, and the Convention on the Rights of the Child, and on Discrimination Against Women. In recounting "The Principles of Conservatism," the flagship Heritage Foundation declared that "international agreements and international organizations should not infringe on American's constitutional rights, nor should they diminish American sovereignty." In 2000, Jean Kirkpatrick, President Reagan's former UN Ambassador, wrote that "foreign governments and their leaders, and more than a few activists at home, seek to constrain and control American power by means of elaborate multilateral processes, global arrangements, and U.N. treaties that limit both our capacity to govern ourselves and act abroad."

Donald Trump dubbed himself an "America First" leader who chose "independence and cooperation over global governance, control and domination." Yet, he shattered the conservative tradition of protecting U.S. sovereignty. As a candidate and president, Trump failed to protect America from the foreign meddling that presents a far more serious threat to sovereignty than conventions against sex discrimination, arms trafficking, or child abuse. He repudiated the tradition from Washington to Obama that refused to tolerate such interference.

On July 27, 2016, candidate Trump said, "Russia, if you're listening, I hope you're able to find the 30,000 emails [of Hillary Clinton] that are missing. I think you will probably be rewarded mightily by our press. Let's see if that happens." For the first time in history, a presidential candidate solicited a foreign power to help him win an election by committing a felony, in this case hacking into a private email server. Russia listened. Soon after, Russian agents sent malicious links to email accounts associated with Hillary Clinton. Trump said that he was only "joking," but apparently Russian President Vladimir Putin has no sense of humor.

Two years later, President Trump, who rarely journeyed abroad, embarked on his most heralded foreign venture, for a summit meeting with Putin in Helsinki, Finland's capital. After a private meeting (with notes seized by the president), Trump and Putin appeared in a joint press conference with the eyes of the world upon them. Like President Gerald Ford, when he famously said in a 1976 presidential debate that "there is no Soviet domination of Eastern Europe," Trump privileged Kremlin propagandists above his own intelligence and national security teams. A journalist asked Trump if he would denounce Russia's interference in America's 2016 presidential election. Trump responded that "my people came to me, [Director of National Intelligence] Dan Coats came to me and some others, they said they think it's Russia. I have President Putin. He just said it's not Russia. I will say this: I don't see any reason why it *would* be" (emphasis added).

Trump then praised Putin for an offer to investigate the Kremlin's own interference in American politics. Putin made "an incredible offer," Trump said. "He offered to have the people working on the case come [to Russia] and work with their investigators. . . . I think that's an incredible offer. OK?" So much for sovereignty.

Trump's pandering appalled his usual Republican allies. Senator Lindsey Graham of South Carolina said the president had "missed an opportunity . . . to firmly hold Russia accountable for 2016 meddling." Senator Tom Cotton of Arkansas said, "Vladimir Putin is a committed adversary of the United States. In the last few years alone, Russia meddled in our presidential campaign, violated arms-control treaties with the United States, invaded Ukraine, assassinated political opponents in the United Kingdom, made common cause with Iran in propping up Bashar al-Assad's outlaw regime in Syria, and cheated not only in the Olympics, but even in the Paralympics."

Unlike Ford, who stood by his claim, Trump tried to play it both ways by saying that he had misspoken in Helsinki. "I said the word 'would' instead of 'wouldn't,'" Trump said in a prepared statement. "The sentence should have been, I don't see any reason why it wouldn't be Russia." This revision of yesterday's history not only clashes with his deference to Putin in Helsinki, but, as usual, Trump went off script to muddy his waters. "Could be other people also, there's a lot of people out there," he said.

Trump cared not that Putin had sown chaos and division in America, interfered with an election, and sapped people's confidence in U.S. democracy. He cared only that Russia's sweeping and systematic intervention in the 2016 election had discredited Clinton and strengthened his candidacy. Special Counsel Robert Mueller did not uncover a criminal conspiracy between Trump and Russia, partly because members of Trump's team had destroyed evidence. Key witnesses, including

President Trump, failed to cooperate and tell the truth. Yet, Mueller found that Trump's campaign had welcomed and exploited Russian interference.

Whether a criminal conspiracy existed or not, the Trump campaign had colluded with the Russians. Russia's "information war" faithfully followed Trump's strategy. They gleaned information and guidance from "unwitting" local Republican activists and wittingly from the Trump campaign chair, Paul Manafort. He provided inside information about the campaign to Ukrainian Konstantin Kilimnik, Manafort's associate when they both worked for pro-Russian interests in Ukraine. Kilimnik, who served as a Russian agent, passed this information on to the Russian Intelligence Services. A bipartisan report from the Senate Intelligence Committee called Manafort a "grave counterintelligence threat."

Mueller and other researchers uncovered more than one hundred contacts between Trump campaign associates and Russia-linked operatives, compared to zero for Clinton's campaign. Contacts continued after July 19, 2016, when the FBI informed Trump about Russian efforts to infiltrate his campaign and asked him to report any Russian openings to the bureau. The Senate report contradicted Trump in finding that "Trump did, in fact, speak with [Roger] Stone about WikiLeaks and with members of his campaign about Stone's access to WikiLeaks on multiple occasions." The Russians had used WikiLeaks as their conduit for stolen Democratic emails. Trump mentioned WikiLeaks an average of more than five times per day during the final month of the 2016 campaign.

No reports from the Trump campaign reached the FBI. When confronted with media coverage of Russian contacts, Trump associates followed Nixon's Watergate playbook by lying. On June 9, 2016, at Trump Tower, Donald Trump Jr., Paul Manafort, and Jared Kushner met on behalf of the Trump campaign with Kremlin-connected Russians. According to email evidence, a Russian contact set the meeting up "to provide the Trump campaign with some official documents and information that would incriminate Hillary." This "is part of Russia and its government's support for Mr. Trump," he said. The Trump team participants claimed they learned nothing useful from the Russians, although details of the meeting remain murky. In March 2017, nine months after the Trump Tower meeting, Donald Trump Jr. falsely told the *New York Times*, "Did I meet with people that were Russian? I'm sure, I'm sure I did. But none that were set up. None that I can think of at the moment. And certainly none that I was representing the campaign in any way, shape or form."

Russia had previously approached candidates with offers of help to win the presidency. But prior candidates rebuffed the Kremlin. In January 1960, Soviet ambassador Mikhail A. Menshikov delivered a message to former Democratic presidential candidate Adlai Stevenson that he said came from the Soviet Premier Nikita Khrushchev himself. He said that the Russians favored Stevenson as the next American president. "We believe that Mr. Stevenson is more of a realist than others and is likely to understand Soviet anxieties and purposes," Menshikov said. "We in our hearts favor him." He offered to have the Soviet press assist Stevenson through praise or criticism, at the American's discretion.

An appalled Stevenson bluntly told the ambassador that such meddling was "highly improper, indiscreet, and dangerous." He expressed his "grave misgivings about the propriety or wisdom of any interference, direct or indirect, in the American election." To discourage further Russian interference, Stevenson informed James Reston, a prominent *New York Times* columnist, about the Soviet overture. Reston wrote that the Russians were showing "both a keen interest in the United States election and appalling ignorance of the dangers in commenting on it." He warned that Americans would not tolerate any foreign interference in their democracy.

In 1968, the Soviets feared that the fiercely anti-communist Republican candidate Richard Nixon would win the presidency. Under instructions from the Kremlin, the Russian ambassador Anatoly Dobrynin approached Nixon's opponent, Vice President Hubert Humphrey. He offered Humphrey financial assistance from the Soviets. Dobrynin later said that Humphrey "knew at once what was going on," and immediately declined the offer.

Ironically, while Humphrey spurned Russian help, Nixon had colluded with a foreign nation to help him defeat the vice president. Nixon knew that he would lose the closely fought election if North and South Vietnam reached a peace deal before Election Day. Through his agent, Anna Chennault (aka the "Dragon Lady"), the widow of Claire Lee Chennault, leader of the Flying Tigers in China during World War II, Nixon told the South Vietnamese leadership to stall peace negotiations.

He sent the message that he would win the election and get them a better deal.

While any deal might have been a long shot even without Chennault's intervention, Nixon had tried to thwart peace in Vietnam, potentially costing thousands of American and Asian lives. Nixon's biographer John A. Farrell said that Nixon's "apparently criminal behavior" during the campaign "may be more reprehensible than anything Nixon did in Watergate," because of "the human lives at stake and the decade of carnage that followed in Southeast Asia."

President Johnson, who had wiretapped Nixon's telephone, overheard Nixon declare that "we're going to say to Hanoi, 'I [Nixon] can make a better deal than he [Johnson] has, because I'm fresh and new, and I don't have to demand as much as he does in the light of past positions,'" and Anna Chennault's "warning them to not get pulled in on this Johnson [peace] move." In a conversation with Republican Senate Minority Leader Everett Dirksen, Johnson said, "This is treason . . . that they're contacting a foreign power in the middle of a war." Johnson never revealed Nixon's alleged betrayal, perhaps because he believed Nixon would win anyway and did not want to risk a national crisis. President Obama made the same mistake by not fully exposing and responding to Russian interference in the 2016 election before the verdict was in. "Better three hours too soon," Shakespeare wrote, "than a minute too late."

In 2016, President Putin, like his Soviet predecessors, had good reasons for intervening in America's presidential election. He believed that contrary to Hillary Clinton, Donald Trump would not stand in the way of his imperial ambitions for Russia. He expected Trump to lift the sanctions that President Barack Obama had imposed on Russia after it seized Crimea from Ukraine. During the campaign, Trump said he would "look into" recognizing Crimea as Russian territory and lifting the sanctions. Trump said that NATO was outdated and that he would consider withdrawing the United States if it were not restructured. He hailed Putin as a stronger leader than Obama and defended him against charges that he ordered the assassinations of journalists and dissidents. "We're going to have a great relationship with Putin and Russia," Trump pledged.

In some ways, Trump failed to fully deliver for Russia as Putin might have expected. National Security Advisor Michael Flynn's lies about his talks with the Russian ambassador and his subsequent indictment for perjury made it perilous politically for Trump to lift the Russia sanctions. Trump imposed some limited new sanctions on Russian companies and individuals. He sold Javelin anti-tank missiles to Ukraine, although they remained in storage and would not stop a Russian attack.

Overall, however, Putin received a bountiful return on his investment in Trump, with almost no collateral damage to the Kremlin. The president resisted bipartisan efforts to impose far more stringent and effective sanctions on Russia. His opposition stymied comprehensive legislation sponsored in 2019 by Republican Senator Lindsey Graham that would have tightened protections against hacking. It would have imposed new sanctions to deter Russia from again intervening in American democracy and expanded reporting requirements on Russian economic, military, and political activities. It would have permanently reauthorized legislation that allows a president to sanction foreigners who violate human rights.

Trump advanced Putin's imperial goals in the autocrat's two main targets, Syria and Ukraine. Trump withheld American military aid and held a White House meeting to coerce the new Ukrainian president into investigating Trump's political opponent and promote the Russian propaganda line that it was Ukraine, not Russia, that meddled in the 2016 election. On October 7, 2019, Trump gave Putin a priceless gift for the autocrat's sixty-seventh birthday. He withdrew American forces from northern Syria, which ceded control over Syria to Putin and his murderous ally, President Bashar al-Assad. Without anything in return from Putin, Trump delivered a prize that the Russians had long sought: a sure foothold in the Middle East. "Why is Russia returning to the Middle East?" asked Eugene Rumor, the director of the Russia and Eurasia Program at the Carnegie Endowment for International Peace. Rumor's answer: "The Middle East is the crossroads of the world, where tradition, interests, and political ambition all mandate an active Russian presence."

Trump ordered the removal of some 12,500 American troops from Germany, which served as the sturdy redoubt against Russia's aggression in Europe. Bipartisan leaders in Congress denounced this decision, which seriously weakened the NATO alliance and only benefited President Putin. Retired Admiral Jim Stavridis, formerly the top commander in Europe and NATO, said, "Abruptly pulling 12,500 troops out of Germany (to put half of them in countries who spend *less* on defense) doesn't make sense financially, hurts NATO solidarity overall, and is a gift to Putin."

When credible evidence indicated that Putin had arranged the poisoning of his chief opposition leader, Alexei Navalny, Trump failed to join German Chancellor Angela Merkel and British Prime Minister Boris Johnson in confronting Russia. Instead, after a long delay, he said, "I don't know exactly what happened." He added, "I do get along with President Putin" and gratuitously deflected attention to his usual scapegoat, China. He said, "China at this point is probably a nation that you should be talking about much more so than Russia, because the things that China is doing are far worse."

While Trump delighted in verbally thrashing China, an eyewitness account by his former National Security Advisor John Bolton revealed that Trump had colluded with Chinese leader Xi Jinping to help with his reelection. In his memoir, *The Room Where It Happened*, Bolton related that in a June 29, 2019, talk with Xi, Trump "stunningly turned the conversation to the coming US presidential election, alluding to China's economic capability to affect the ongoing campaigns, pleading with Xi to ensure he'd win. He stressed the importance of farmers, and increased Chinese purchases of soybeans and wheat in the electoral outcome." Bolton said, "I would print Trump's exact words, but the government's prepublication review process has decided otherwise."

In the summer of 2020, the press revealed that American intelligence services had uncovered evidence that Russian government operatives had offered bounties to Taliban militants in Afghanistan for killing American soldiers. Although the intelligence was far from definitive, Trump did not convene his national security advisors to get to the bottom of this allegation or confront President Putin. Instead, he did nothing. He did nothing again when credible reports emerged that Russia had hacked into America's programs for developing a coronavirus vaccine. In a call with Putin in late July 2020, Trump did not mention either one of these issues. For political enemies, real and imaginary, Trump channeled his hero, General George S. Patton, who famously said, "There is only attack and attack and attack some more." But in the face of President Putin's real threats to the sovereignty and security of the United States, Trump became Benedict Arnold and surrendered.

Bill Browder, an authority on Putin's Russia, said, "Putin is in the business of just pushing all boundaries, and if he can get away with stuff, if he can do things and succeed then he will carry on doing it." With no retaliation from a supine President Trump, Putin pushed on, hard. Shortly after the 2020 elections, the U.S. intelligence community discovered that Kremlin operatives had hacked computers of many private companies and departments and agencies of the government, including the Pentagon and the Nuclear Security Administration, which controls our nuclear arsenal. The federal Cybersecurity and Infrastructure Security Agency warned that the breach "poses a grave risk" to government "as well as critical infrastructure entities and other private sector organizations."

Republican Senator Marco Rubio of Florida called it "the gravest cyber intrusion in our history," and veteran journalist Mike Allen said, "If this had been a physical attack on America's secrets, we could be at war." But physical attacks, wrote General Valery Gerasimov, chief of the general staff of the Russian Federation, are less lethal than modern cyberwarfare through which "a perfectly thriving state can, in a matter of months and even days, be transformed into an arena of fierce armed conflict, become a victim of foreign intervention, and sink into a web of chaos, humanitarian catastrophe, and civil war."

Tom Bossert, who had previously headed the Trump administration's cybersecurity efforts, agreed that "President Trump is on the verge of leaving behind a federal government, and perhaps a large number of major industries, compromised by the Russian government. He must use whatever leverage he can muster to protect the United States and severely punish the Russians." Bossert's plea fell on deaf ears.

On December 19, 2020, the day after Secretary of State Mike Pompeo, a Trump loyalist, confirmed that the breach was "very significant" and "pretty clearly that it was the Russians," Trump again waved the white flag. Without evidence, the president downplayed the attack and deflected blame from Russia to China and from intelligence reports to the media, his favored whipping boys. "Cyber Hack is far greater in the Fake News Media than in actuality," he tweeted, "everything is well under control." He added, "Russia, Russia, Russia is the priority chant when anything happens because Lamestream is, for mostly financial reasons, petrified of discussing the possibility that it may be China (it may!)." Trump then could not help but add that this overblown hack might somehow explain his election defeat. "There could also have been a hit on our ridiculous voting machines during the election, which is now obvious that I won big," he said. Rice University historian Douglas Brinkley said, "the big question" for American history is no longer who killed JFK, but "what in the world does Russia have on Donald Trump that he is willing to grovel in front of Putin?"

During the uproar over the alleged Russian bounty payments, Trump's allies in the Senate stripped from the National Defense Authorization Act a requirement for presidential campaigns to report offers of foreign election assistance, which Trump did not view as a problem. During his June 2019 interview, George Stephanopoulos asked Trump whether he would accept damaging information about his opponents from foreign nations. Trump responded, "I think you might want to listen, there isn't anything wrong with listening. If somebody called from a country, Norway, [and said] 'we have information on your opponent'—oh, I think I'd want to hear it. It's not an interference, they have information—I think I'd take it." He added that there is nothing wrong with taking "oppo research" from foreign nations. When Stephanopoulos noted that, according to FBI Director Christopher Wray, candidates should report to the FBI any solicitation from foreigners, Trump disagreed. "The FBI director is wrong, because frankly, it doesn't happen like that in life," Trump said.

Unlike the hacking operations of 2016, Russian meddling in the 2020 presidential campaign focused on influencing the election by promoting false narratives and deceptive claims beneficial to Trump. The Democrats had strengthened their online security. Federal Cybersecurity Director Christopher Krebs had worked with state and local governments to secure their election infrastructure. Neither the Russians nor another foreign adversary sabotaged the election process or outcome in any state, another indication that voting was secure and fair in 2020. Trump fired Krebs after he attested to the security of the election.

A comprehensive report by a unanimous U.S intelligence community on March 10, 2021, confirmed with high confidence that Russia, at the explicit direction of President Putin, engaged in a massive influence campaign to help Donald Trump, denigrate Joe Biden, and sabotage American democracy. The "Russian leaders viewed President Biden's potential election as disadvantageous to Russian interests and this drove their efforts to undermine his candidacy," the report concluded.

Another Trump administration, the Russians believed, would best serve their interests.

The confluence between misinformation from the Russians and the Trump campaign was no accident. The intelligence community uncovered collusion between Russian intelligence agents and Trump associates, despite warnings by the FBI to avoid contact with foreign entities or agents. The Kremlin found a receptive audience among Trump's loyalists in 2020, because Putin and Trump shared common goals. They both sought to secure the president's reelection, to exploit social and political division in the United States, and to challenge America's democratic values and traditions.

Kremlin operatives influenced willing Trump loyalists to disseminate Russian lies about Biden and the Democrats. The report concluded with high confidence that Moscow used "*proxies linked to Russian intelligence to push influence narratives—including misleading or unsubstantiated allegations against President Biden—to US media organizations, US officials, and prominent US individuals, including some close to former President Trump and his administration*" (emphasis in original). It found that "Russian proxies met with and provided material to Trump administration-linked figures" and engaged in "direct outreach to senior US Government officials."

The report noted that Russian intelligence deployed two of their active agents, Paul Manafort's former associate Konstantin Kilimnik and Andriy Derkach, to use "prominent US persons and media conduits to launder their narratives to US officials and audiences." The United States has sanctioned both Kilimnik and Derkach. Trump's personal attorney, Rudy Giuliani, had met with Derkach to aid in the lawyer's smear campaign against Joe Biden and his son Hunter. Giuliani and Derkach appeared in a One America News (OAN) documentary entitled *The Ukraine Hoax: Impeachment, Biden Cash, and Mass Murder with Michael Caputo*, which aired in January 2020.

OAN boasted that Derkach had given Giuliani access to hundreds of pages of Biden-related documents. The report cites this program, which echoed Kremlin propaganda about Ukraine and the Bidens, as a product of Russian intelligence. "Russian proxies," the report read, "made contact with established US media figures and helped produce a documentary that aired on a US television network in late January 2020." Trump rewarded Caputo by appointing him as spokesperson for

Health and Human Services. He then censured, delayed, and altered scientific reports to downplay the impact of the pandemic and the need for testing.

The Russians promoted a central theme of the Trump campaign "by denigrating mail-in ballots, highlighting alleged irregularities, and accusing the Democratic Party of fraud." The Russians further "promoted former President Trump and his commentary, including repeating his political messaging on the election results; the presidential campaign; debates; the impeachment inquiry; and, as the election neared, US domestic crises." After the election, the Kremlin amplified Trump's big lie about Democratic fraud and a stolen result. It advanced "narratives questioning the election results and disparaging President Biden and the Democratic Party."

The intelligence community concluded with high confidence that China considered, but "did not attempt to influence the presidential election outcome." Rather, "China sought stability in its relationship with the United States and did not view either election outcome as being advantageous enough for China to risk blowback if caught." Unlike its conclusions about China, the intelligence community found with high confidence that Iran "carried out a multi-pronged covert influence campaign intended to undercut former President Trump's reelection prospects—although without directly promoting his rivals." However, Iranian interference did not approach the scope and depth of the Russian operation.

The report warned that even though Putin had failed to secure a complaisant president, the Kremlin could still win by sabotaging democracy, pitting Americans against one another, and promoting Russian-favored candidates in future elections. It concluded that "Moscow will continue election influence efforts to further its longstanding goal of weakening Washington because the Kremlin has long deemed that a weakened United States would be less likely to pursue assertive foreign and security policies abroad and more open to geopolitical bargains with Russia."

The Trump administration did not deter or discourage Moscow's interference in the election. Instead, it withheld the Department of Homeland Security's report documenting Russian-propagated rumors about Biden's health, which Trump retweeted. H. R. McMaster, Trump's former national security advisor, said that Trump was "aid-ing and abetting Putin's efforts by not being direct about this. This sustained campaign of disruption, disinformation and denial is aided by any leader who doesn't acknowledge it." A January 2021 report by the intelligence community ombudsmen found that during the campaign, "analysis on foreign election interference was delayed, distorted or obstructed out of concern over policymaker reactions or for political reasons." Despite knowing better from their access to intelligence reports, Trump, Attorney General William Barr, and Director of National Intelligence John Ratcliff diverted attention from Russia to China. When the CIA warned the president about Giuliani's dealings with a Russian agent, Trump did nothing. On the contrary, he retweeted some of the propaganda that Derkach had released. Throughout the campaign, Trump recycled Russian propaganda in rallies and tweets.

When Trump supporters stormed the Capitol on January 6, 2021, Russian leaders cheered. "The electoral system in the U.S. is archaic and doesn't meet modern democratic standards, creates the possibility for various violations, and the American media has become an instrument of political infighting," said Russian Foreign Ministry spokesperson Maria Zakharova. "The celebration of democracy is over" in the United States, proclaimed Konstantin Kosachev, head of the foreign affairs committee in Russia's Federation Council. "America no longer forges that path, and consequently has lost its right to define it. Much less force it on others."

## THE FIX: TIGHTEN AND UPDATE THE LAWS

Only the force of law, not the self-restraint of candidates and presidents, can protect America's democracy from malefactors abroad. Congress should require a federal candidate or campaign organization to report any solicitation from a foreign nation or its agents to the FBI. Failure to comply should be a criminal offense. New laws should require a presidential nominee to disclose all business arrangements or negotiations with foreign nations.

Congress should impose mandatory sanctions against any country that the Director of National Intelligence identifies as interfering in an American election. Offenses should include hacking into private or government computers, registration rolls, or election machines; releasing damaging information on any candidate; or organizing a disinformation campaign. None of this means that foreign nationals cannot have preferences in U.S. elections or express their opinions via regular media channels. But these new safeguards would help put an end to the covert and anti-democratic influence that foreign actors have exerted on American democracy. Congress should impose similar sanctions against governments that hack into U.S. government computers for any reason, not just to interfere in a U.S. election.

It is time to update the campaign finance legislation of the Watergate era. Current law prohibits candidates or campaigns from soliciting or taking "anything of value" from foreigners, directly or indirectly. Still, the problem lies in the meaning of "value." The *Mueller Report* exonerated Trump campaign officials from violating this law, in part because prosecutors could not decide whether the valuation of "opposition research" from Russia met the threshold of $25,000 for a felony violation. In fact, opposition research is pure gold for presidential campaigns, for which they spend millions of dollars. Candidates should not be able to hide behind an ambiguous provision of law.

As proposed by Ellen Weintraub, the chair of the Federal Elections Commission, a fortified law would clarify the definition of a campaign contribution to include "non-public" information given at no cost or "below market value" and that would cost a campaign a "non-trivial" amount to obtain. It would prohibit the solicitation or receipt of "any information that could be used to blackmail or otherwise compromise a candidate for federal office, regardless of the source of the information."

Congress's final step should be to defend America's registration rolls and voting technology. Following the contested presidential election of 2000, Congress passed the Help America Vote Act (HAVA) to improve the conduct of elections and broaden voter access. Congress should revise, update, and fully fund HAVA to mandate a verified paper trail for all voting machines, postelection audits, and cybersecurity protections for registration records and voting infrastructure.

## · 4 ·

# A Presidency Built on Lies

## *Reclaiming Truth*

> The whole texture of facts in which we spend our daily
> life is always in danger of being perforated by single lies
> or torn to shreds by organized lying.
>
> —Political philosopher Hannah Arendt, 1967

$\mathscr{T}$he black helicopters are coming. Filled with armed men in black, they are the vanguard of a shadowy force of globalists ready to occupy the streets of America in a conspiracy with manipulated Democrats and liberals. The far-right fringe of the 1970s militia movement perpetrated this fantasy, the same fanatics who denied the Holocaust and warned against a Jewish plot to conquer the world. Among sane Americans, the invasion of black helicopters has become the subject of bad jokes or fictitious memes for movies, songs, and video games.

The lyrics of a punk-rock song by Lard reflects the wacky essence of the black helicopter conspiracy:

> What's that noise?
> It's those helicopters again
> See 'em in the sky, they're always black
> What does that tell you, huh?. . . .
> To take our guns
> They're trying to take our guns
> Feminazis and eco-terrorists
> I'm not making this up.

Only the looniest extremists clung to the myth of invading black helicopters. That is, until none other than the president of the United

States revived a close facsimile. In an interview with Fox News host Laura Ingraham on August 31, 2020, Trump warned with a straight face that "people that you've never heard of, people that are in the dark shadows" were manipulating his Democratic opponent, Joe Biden. This was too much even for the ever-loyal Ingraham. "What does that mean?" she asked. "That sounds like conspiracy theory. 'Dark shadows,' what is that?"

Undaunted, Trump plowed on. "No. People that you haven't heard of," he said. "They're people that are controlling the streets. We had somebody get on a plane from a certain city this weekend, and in the plane, it was almost completely loaded with thugs wearing these dark uniforms, black uniforms with gear and this and that."

"Where—where was this?" Ingraham asked.

"I'll tell you sometime, but it's under investigation right now," Trump responded. "But they came from a certain city, and this person was coming to the Republican National Convention . . . a lot of people were on the plane to do big damage." The next day, Trump doubled down on his version of the black helicopter conspiracy but reversed the plane's direction. He now said it was going not to Washington, but "from Washington to wherever." Trump claimed that he had a witness. "A person was on a plane . . . and what happened is the entire plane filled up with the looters, the anarchists, rioters, people looking for trouble. . . . Maybe they'll speak to you, maybe they won't." Trump's witness never emerged, and no invaders appeared.

Trump's channeling of the black helicopter myth has meaning and intent. It complements his efforts to make the most fringe ideas mainstream and portray himself as beset by dark conspirators. "'Deep state' actors [federal bureaucrats], globalists, bankers, Islamists, and establishment Republicans," are working to destroy Trump and America, wrote loyalist Richard Higgins. "If you don't fight like hell," Trump warned, "you're not going to have a country anymore."

Trump's prolific lying is the indispensable predicate for his assault upon democracy and his shift toward autocracy. A president who replaces truth with self-serving fiction may claim that the Constitution gives him unlimited power and absolute immunity from congressional oversight. He can deny foreign interference on his behalf in elections and claim that an unleashed pandemic is under control. He can disrupt the peaceful transfer of power by inventing the myth of a stolen election. Political philosopher Sissela Bok wrote that "public officials, above all, can have a uniquely deleterious effect on trust. When they act so as to undermine trust, this cuts at the roots of democracy."

"All administrations lie, but what we are seeing here" from Donald Trump "is an attack on credibility itself," said former conservative talk show host Charlie Sykes. "Trying to pick the most notable lies from Donald Trump's presidency is like trying to pick the most notable pieces of junk from the town dump. There's just so much ugly garbage to sift through," said CNN fact checker Daniel Dale. His counterparts at the *Washington Post*, after documenting some thirty thousand false and misleading statements from President Trump—more than all prior presidents combined—gave up late in his presidency. With Trump's deceptions surpassing fifty per day, the fact checkers could not keep up.

Other presidents have lied, at times egregiously. Both the president and the American people have paid a price. In 1960, Premier Nikita Khrushchev claimed to have shot down a U.S. U-2 spy plane over Soviet territory. President Dwight Eisenhower fell into Khrushchev's trap when his administration denied that the United States flew surveillance flights over Russia. Then Khrushchev sprung the trap by producing the aircraft's wreckage and its captured pilot, Francis Gary Powers. Unlike Trump, Eisenhower had shame. "I would like to resign," a despondent president told his secretary. The U-2 fiasco sabotaged a summit meeting with Khrushchev. It contributed to John F. Kennedy's hairline victory over Eisenhower's vice president, Richard Nixon, in the upcoming presidential election.

In the 1960s, President Lyndon Johnson lied about progress in the Vietnam War, even making up body counts of the enemy. Stories about his deceptions fueled the so-called credibility gap, which soured members of his own party on Johnson. Under pressure from opposition Democrats, Johnson withdrew from consideration for reelection in 1968. Ironically, Johnson had likely handed the presidency to Richard Nixon, who defeated Vice President Hubert Humphrey in the general election.

In an August 29, 1972, press conference, President Nixon falsely claimed that an investigation by White House counsel John Dean cleared everyone in his administration of involvement "in this very bizarre incident" of the Watergate break-in. "We are doing everything we can to take this incident [seriously] and not to cover it up," he said. In his one bow to the truth, Nixon ironically added, "What really hurts is if you try to cover it up." Nixon's lies survived the presidential election of 1972, but not his second term, when he resigned to avoid impeachment by the U.S. House and conviction in the Senate.

Upon taking office, President Nixon intensified the bombing of Cambodia that President Johnson had initiated. "I want everything that can fly to go in there and crack the hell out of them," Nixon said to his National Security Advisor, Henry Kissinger. The United States dropped a greater tonnage of TNT on this small nation than on all its enemies during World War II. The president covered up this illicit bombing with lies. The bombing of Cambodia is "the best-kept secret of the war!" Nixon told Senate hawk John Stennis of Mississippi in April 1970. Days later, Nixon said at a press conference that his policy "has been to scrupulously respect the neutrality of the Cambodian people." Once the bombing became public, Nixon draped himself in the justification of "national security," even though he had admitted in handwritten notes on a confidential memo that the cumulative impact of all his bombings in Southeast Asia was "zilch." Investigations of the illicit bombing campaign diminished the president's public standing and led Congress to enact over his veto the War Powers Act of 1973, which limited, on paper, a president's war-making authority.

President Ronald Reagan lied to the American people about not trading arms for hostages with the terrorist state of Iran. With his approval rating plummeting, Reagan delivered a televised address to rescue his presidency. Reagan deftly slipped away from his deception. "A few months ago, I told the American people that I did not trade arms for hostages," Reagan said. "My heart and my best intentions still tell me that is true, but the facts and evidence tell me it is not." Although Reagan's explanation made no logical sense, the American people bought it, and his approval rating climbed. His lie, however, added to public skepticism about the presidency that prior executives had already damaged with lies about Vietnam and the Watergate scandal.

President Bill Clinton lied to the American people and under oath to a grand jury about his sexual relations with White House intern Monica Lewinsky. His lies led to scathing criticism from fellow Democrats, to calls for his resignation from some major newspapers, and to his impeachment by a Republican Congress. Although the Senate acquitted Clinton, the impeachment scandal cast a pall over his presidency. It contributed to his vice president, Al Gore, losing the presidency to George W. Bush in 2000.

To justify his 2003 invasion of Iraq, President George W. Bush and his aides distorted and cherry-picked intelligence about Iraqi dictator Saddam Hussein's weapons of mass destruction. Convinced that he must scare Americans to death to justify invading a nation unrelated to the 9/11 attacks, Bush starkly warned, "Facing clear evidence of peril, we cannot wait for the final proof—the smoking gun—that could come in the form of a mushroom cloud." Premier Republican strategist and Bush aide Karl Rove justified the president's lying. "The reality-based community" of people who "believe that solutions emerge from your judicious study of discernible reality" are passe, he said. "That's not the way the world really works anymore. We're an empire now, and when we act, we create our own reality. And while you're studying that reality—judiciously, as you will—we'll act again, creating other new realities, which you can study too."

One critic charged that President Bush "got us into the war with lies." The U.S. House should have pushed "to impeach Bush and get him out of office, which, which, personally, I think would have been a wonderful thing." The critic was Donald J. Trump. Even when inspectors determined that Saddam had no chemical or biological weapons and had long ago abandoned his nuclear weapons program, a rudderless war continued. Its drag contributed to Republican losses of Congress in 2006 and the presidency in 2008.

President Barack Obama repeatedly said that under his Affordable Care Act (Obamacare), people could choose to keep their current health care plan. Yet, millions of Americans found that their insurance plans did not comply with the requirements of the act. What PolitiFact would call the "lie of the year" diminished public support. Opinion of Obamacare remained generally negative until after Obama left office.

But Trump's lies are unlike those of any prior president. In building a presidency on lies, Trump has shredded reality itself. No lie is too small for Donald Trump: inflating the size of his inauguration crowds, claiming to have won Michigan's "Man of the Year" award or holding the record in *Time* magazine covers. In his most revealing small lie, Trump said that, like the Red Sea parting for the Israelites, the forecasted rain for his 2016 inauguration held off until he finished his address. Yet, as everyone watching knew, the rain came down just as he began speaking. "These constant little lies are conditioning, they're meant to sort of condition their followers to just go along with whatever they say," said information analyst David Roberts. "And once you've got that, then it's like, off to the autocratic races."

Trump's "off to the races" big lies had devastating consequences for the American people. Trump cynically lied about the COVID-19 pandemic to boost his prospects for reelection. In a conversation that interviewer Bob Woodward taped, Trump said that the coronavirus was "more deadly than even your strenuous flus" and was spread through "the air, you just breathe the air and that's how it's passed." Yet, Trump repeatedly said that the virus was "under control," was no more deadly than the flu, and would soon disappear. He mocked the wearing of masks and reveled in largely mask-free mass rallies. At the final presidential debate on October 22, 2020, Trump said, "we are rounding the turn, it's going away" on the pandemic, even as cases, hospitalizations, and deaths were surging. As of debate day, 222,538 Americans had died of COVID-19. On the last day of Trump's term, less than three months later, the death toll had nearly doubled to 405,212.

An analysis completed in March 2021 by Andrew Atkeson, an economics professor at the University of California, Los Angeles, estimated that more than three hundred thousand U.S. COVID-19 fatalities could have been avoided if the United States had adopted widespread mask, social distancing, and testing protocols while awaiting the development and distribution of vaccines.

Former White House coronavirus response coordinator Dr. Deborah Birx had praised Trump for being "so attentive to the scientific literature." But she agreed in a March 2021 interview that hundreds of thousands of deaths "could have been mitigated or decreased substantially" with a better response in the early stages of the pandemic. "I was marginalized every day. I mean, that is no question. The majority of the people in the White House did not take this seriously," said Birx.

Other admissions by former Trump officials, also issued after he left office, confirm the deadly propagation of lies about the pandemic. Admiral Brett P. Giroir, the testing czar, said in March 2021 that the administration had lied to the public about the availability of testing. "When we said there were millions of tests—there weren't, right?" he said. "There were components of the test available, but not the full deal." Dr. Robert R. Redfield, the former director of the Centers for

Disease Control and Prevention, accused President Trump's health secretary, Alex M. Azar III, and the secretary's leadership team of pressuring him multiple times to revise scientific reports. "Now, he may deny that, but it's true," Redfield said. Dr. Stephen K. Hahn, the former commissioner of the Food and Drug Administration, said his relationship with Mr. Azar had grown "strained" after the health secretary revoked the agency's power to regulate coronavirus tests. "That was a line in the sand for me," Dr. Hahn said.

The pandemic lies had the sole purpose of stroking the ego of one man—Donald Trump—and advancing his political ambitions. But the deadly deceptions were not limited to Trump. Their propagation required collaborators like White House aides Dr. Azar, Dr. Giroir, and Dr. Scott Atlas, a radiologist with no credentials in epidemiology or virology, who fed misinformation to Trump. The lies required enablers like Dr. Birx, Dr. Redfield, and Dr. Hahn, who told the truth much too late. Dr. Megan L. Ranney, associate professor of health services, policy, and practice at Brown University, lamented that "for months as the calamity worsened, she [Dr. Birx] let Trump's lies go unchecked on the public stage. The harm was irrevocable." The lesson, she said, is, "Don't hesitate to blow the whistle. Don't keep quiet when something is really wrong. The AIDS activists were right decades ago: Silence = death."

Trump's big lies about climate change justified his strangulation of prior efforts to combat this existential threat to humanity's well-being and survival. "We've lost very important time on climate change, which we can ill afford," said Richard Newell, president of Resources for the Future, a nonpartisan energy and environmental research organization. "There is severe damage." Trump misled Americans about climate science, despite knowing better.

On December 6, 2009, on the eve of UN Climate Talks in Copenhagen, business leaders wrote an open letter to President Barack Obama, saying, "If we fail to act now [on climate change], it is scientifically irrefutable that there will be catastrophic and irreversible consequences for humanity and our planet." It added, "Investing in a clean energy economy will drive state-of-the-art technologies that will spur economic growth, create new energy jobs, and increase our energy security, all the while reducing the harmful emissions that are putting our planet at risk." Signatories included Donald J. Trump, Donald

Trump Jr., Eric Trump, and Ivanka Trump. Since 2009, the science has become more irrefutable and the effects of climate change more evident. What changed was Trump's calculation that to succeed in Republican politics, he had to become a climate skeptic or denier.

Following the 2020 election, Trump and his enablers repeatedly lied that this was a "stolen election." They claimed that Trump really won in a landslide, but felonious Democrats stole his victory through massive voter fraud. The lie undermined people's faith in America's democracy and incited his most extreme followers to storm the Capitol to stop Congress from counting electoral votes on January 6, 2021. Ironically, some of the arrested rioters had never bothered to vote in 2020.

After leaving office, Trump advanced another big lie about the Capitol insurrection. In an interview with Fox News on March 25, 2021, he ignored the five dead and the 140 injured policemen. Instead, he claimed that the rioters posed "zero threat." He added that contrary to what Americans saw on television, "some of them went in and they're hugging and kissing the police and the guards, they had great relationships. A lot of the people were waved in, and then they walked in and they walked out." "What you're seeing and what you're reading is not what's happening," Trump had earlier told the public.

In today's digital world, the dangers of lies, especially when issued under the leadership of a president, exceed even the warnings of the prescient George Orwell. The scholarly consensus, wrote Thomas Edsall, in the *New York Times* on February 17, 2021, "no longer celebrates digital media's democratic promise as a voice for ordinary citizens." Instead, "the consensus has shifted to anxiety" that it has fostered "a crisis of knowledge—confounding what is true and what is untrue—eroding the foundations of democracy." Online social media gives lies greater life, range, and impact than in the days of pens and typewriters. Until Twitter suspended Trump's account in the dying days of his presidency, he exploited this platform to spread his lies instantly and repeatedly to more than eighty million followers. "Fake news on Twitter spreads six times faster than true news," said Tristan Harris, the former ethics designer at Google and a featured authority for the documentary film *The Social Dilemma.*

Social media has created insular communities of persons steeped in lies. Unlike face-to-face communities, these virtual gatherings bring people together not by proximity, but only by shared beliefs. "The internet affords environments . . . where they can make common cause with people they would not find in their neighborhood or in face-to-face forums," wrote Nathaniel Persily, a law professor at Stanford University. "In other words, there are shadowy places on the internet where conspiracy communities, like QAnon, or hate groups, can thrive." QAnon is a catchall group for conspiracy theories, particularly the myth that Democrats and their allies are a satanic cult of cannibalistic pedophiles. Even after the insurrection at the Capitol, a Morning Consult poll found that "24 percent of GOP voters who have heard of QAnon say its claims are at least somewhat accurate."

Companies like Twitter, Google, Facebook/Instagram, and YouTube derive their revenue from advertising on their platforms. They surveil people's values, preferences, and behaviors and then use the data for marketing user-specific ads. "If you are not paying for the product, then you are the product," Harris said. "We can have democracy, or we can have a surveillance society, but we cannot have both," warned Shoshana Zuboff, professor emeritus at the Harvard Business School. "This new form of information capitalism aims to predict and modify human behavior as a means to produce revenue and market control." Marketing the product of surveillance "has made internet companies, the richest companies in the history of humanity."

Through a conscious, lucrative design, for-profit, online businesses rely on impersonal computer-driven algorithms to create like-minded communities for micro-targeted advertising. The algorithms are turbocharged designers of what you see and do not see. The data they use to put "people into different groups and segments is much more than demographic," says Saleem Alhabash, co-director of the Media and Advertising Psychology Lab at Michigan State University. "It's the things you interact with, every URL you click on." According to David Carroll, associate professor of media design at the New School, "All of my interactions, my credit card swipes, web searches, locations, my life, they're collected in real time and attached to my identity, giving any buyer direct access to my emotional pulse." He said that "the dream of a connected world" has come "to tear us apart." During the 2016 campaign, an organization called Cambridge Analytica acquired this information for millions of targeted ads and a social media blitz on behalf of the Trump campaign.

Lies must have believers—better still, communities of believers. Why, for example, do tens of millions of Trump followers believe his patent lie about a stolen election in 2020? Why does that lie drive Americans to revolt against their government? The answer is that true believers thrive within an autonomous bubble of "alternative facts." In 2017, NBA star Kyrie Irving emerged from his rabbit hole to proclaim the "alternative fact" that the "the earth is flat." The supposed fact of a round earth, he said, is what some unspecified "they" falsely propagates.

People in the bubble do not weigh "alternative facts" against reliable information. When a politician such as Trump creates an alternate reality, it becomes the reality of another person. Algorithmic island communities reinforce and perpetuate shared beliefs and fantasies, regardless of how eccentric or extreme they are. A study by researchers from Harvard University and the University of Rome found that Facebook communities become "polarized," with "information that strengthens their preferred narrative." Like the end-of-the-world preachers who unabashedly revise their predictions when doomsday fails to arrive on time, true believers are impervious to clashes with reality. In the bubble, fiction becomes truth and truth becomes fiction.

People think they are doing their own research and making discoveries, while algorithms send them to information that reinforces their beliefs and biases. Like a crack addict, they become psychologically and physically dependent on what they look at every day and they cannot escape from. The algorithmic monsters—"digital Frankensteins," in Harris's words—are in control, not people. People "see completely different worlds, because they're based on these computers calculating what's perfect for each of them. Facebook controls our news field," Harris said, "for democracy to be completely for sale where you can reach any mind you want, target a lie to that specific population, and create culture wars." He added, "If we don't agree on what's true, or that there is such a thing as truth, we're toast."

David Roberts writes of a world where "information is evaluated based not on conformity to common standards of evidence or correspondence to a common understanding of the world, but on whether it supports the tribe's values and goals and is vouchsafed by tribal leaders," like Donald Trump. From their insular communities, Republican committees in several states censured GOP legislators for sharing with most Americans the belief that Trump should be impeached and convicted for incitement of insurrection. Wyoming's state committee called for the resignation of Representative Liz Cheney, the third-ranking Republican in the U.S. House. The committee excluded her from fundraising assistance and falsely asserted that "ample evidence" proved that Antifa and Black Lives Matter "instigated" the January 6, 2021, riot. FBI Director Christopher Wray testified in a Senate hearing on March 2, 2021, that "we have not seen, to date, any evidence of anarchist violent extremist or people who subscribe to Antifa in connection with January 6."

Analysts from the International Centre for Counter-Terrorism further explain that the insular "group provides beliefs, values, and norms that can justify the use of otherwise abhorrent behaviors." Given "the similarity of shared beliefs about the world, it is not surprising that these groups often function as ideological bubbles where group members reinforce each other's beliefs and fuel associated collective emotions (for example, anxiety as a result of perceived outgroup threats, and moral outrage)." They found that "over time, communication within such ideological bubbles can lead to a reinforcement and transformation of beliefs to become increasingly more extreme."

Tolerant, reasoned, and evidence-based politics leave followers in Trump-linked communities bored and distracted. Trump alone boosts their energy and excitement. He is the Andrew Jackson of his time, a hero to real Americans, the heirs of the pioneers who made America great and who will make it greater yet. The psychologists George Hagman and Harry Paul explain that Trump's appeal "is simple: tell yourself what you need to hear: tell them what they want to hear, be relentless, keep doing it until it becomes . . . a hypnotic echo chamber." Trump and his followers will "Make 'America Great Again,' a reparative fantasy in which . . . they and their leader triumph over their enemies." A study of the 2016 election by sociologist David Norman Smith found that financial worries did not explain the Trump vote. Rather, voters looked for "a domineering leader who would 'crush evil' and 'get rid of rotten apples' and stand up "against feminists, liberals, immigrants, and minorities."

It is not a stretch that Trump's most fanatical followers who believe that Democrats are Satan worshipers should think they are saving America by storming the Capitol to stop Congress from stealing the election. *New York Times* technology columnist Kevin Roose observes that groups fixated on dangerous fantasies are no longer "some fringe movement," but are "a mass movement of people from every walk of life." Tristan Harris warns, "When technology exceeds human weaknesses, this point being crossed is at the root of addiction, polarization, radicalization."

Social psychologist Richard Koenigsberg explains that in a modern society with diminished face-to-face relations, people shift their psychic energy to the group. "What occurs in the case of the intensely committed nationalist, revolutionary, or totalitarian" is that "*the wish to serve the collectivity becomes the central goal in life.*" He adds that "the fantasies that define political ideas are contained within ordinary structures of culture—in symbolic constructs such as 'the nation,' 'protecting the nation,' 'the enemy,' 'rescuing the nation,' 'defending the border,' etc." Insular communities "give extremists a sense of purpose, community, and—most importantly—self-worth," said Duke Professor Christopher Bail. The reason a movement like QAnon "will catch on like wildfire," said Rachel Bernstein, an authority on cults, "is that it makes people feel connected to something important that other people don't yet know about." Hence QAnon's slogan, "where we go one, we go all."

Conspiracy theories have poisoned marriages, friendships, and families. Eleven family members accused Republican Representative Adam Kinzinger of Illinois, who had voted to impeach Trump, of going "against your Christian principals" (sic) and joining the "'devil's army.'" The Reddit forum QAnonCasualties, for sharing personal stories, had 133,000 followers in February 2021, compared to less than a thousand a year earlier. One woman said that her husband's immersion in Trumpian conspiracy theories had turned him into a "ghost," who is no longer present in their family's life. He made her feel like an "enemy" if she challenged his extreme ideas, "like Tom Hanks being a pedophile." A mother described how "my best friend/daughter" began with the "Pizza Gate conspiracy" and "it just went downhill from there. Conspiracy theory after conspiracy theory," until they stopped seeing each other. "Some days, the pain is unbearable. I just want my family back," she said. Another said, "I've lost most of my family to the QAnon black hole. My dad, stepmom, sister, and multiple aunts/uncles and cousins."

Communities of lies will transcend the Trump presidency. "If we go down the status quo for let's say another twenty years, we probably destroy our civilization through willful ignorance," warned Jaron Lanier, a pioneer of virtual reality. "We probably degrade the world's democracies so that they fall into some sort of bizarre autocratic dysfunction."

## THE FIX: A CODE OF CONDUCT, PERJURY PENALTIES, INSTANT FACT CHECKS, AND THE REGULATION OF SOCIAL MEDIA COMPANIES

We cannot stop presidents and other politicians from lying, but we can make it uncomfortable, even dangerous, for them to do so. Now is the time to apply similar standards to the ethical guidelines for attorneys to candidates and public officials. The gold standard of the American Bar Association's Model Code of Professional Responsibility says that lawyers shall not "make a false statement of fact." They shall not "fail to correct a false statement of material fact or law" or "offer evidence that the lawyer knows to be false."

Congress should establish a voluntary code of ethics for candidates and officeholders, like the ABA code. While not criminal, the code would establish a public standard for judging presidents and other public officials. Congress should authorize an independent ombudsman on truth, like the current inspector general assigned to agencies. For a purpose opposite to Orwell's Ministry of Truth, this official would monitor, fact check, and correct the lies of federal officials.

No future president should escape liability for perjury, which the U.S. Supreme Court has condemned as an "obvious and flagrant affront to the basic concepts of judicial proceedings." Although impeachment is not appropriate for every case of perjury, the Supreme Court has never ruled on the criminal indictment of presidents, and the Watergate grand jury had named President Nixon as an unindicted coconspirator. The Justice Department should revise its guidelines against indicting a sitting president to reflect the Nixon precedent.

A team of researchers at Duke University has developed a technology for automated, real-time fact checking. According to Duke Professor Bill Adair, the creator of PolitiFact, "Right now there's a lot of good political fact checking, but people have to go find it. They have to hear the claim, then look up the claim. What we are trying to do is automate it so that the moment the claim is made by a politician, the fact check automatically pops up on their phone, TV screen or tablet."

The fact checker will not identify all falsehoods, particularly in complex or ambiguous situations. It will catch the most egregious lies, such as Trump's assertions about the coronavirus and the stolen 2020 election.

Online platforms have made some strides against misinformation. Twitter first issued warnings about Trump's false tweets, and then in January 2021, blocked him from his favorite platform, as well as Facebook/Instagram, Snapchat, Reddit, and YouTube. Platforms have blocked thousands of accounts of QAnon and others that propagate false and dangerous conspiracy theories. But Americans cannot rely on self-policing alone. "They're saying they can regulate themselves," said Silicon Valley investor Roger McNamee. "That's just a lie."

Like other businesses, online companies should be regulated in the public interest. A new Social Network Act would focus on transparency and disclosure, while not restricting freedom of expression by imposing liability for content. The act would require online platforms and search engines to reveal how they use personal information and to obtain authorization from individuals and group users, without penalty, for collection. It would mandate "algorithmic transparency," a disclosure requirement that makes the workings of algorithms visible, or transparent. The new law should include similar disclosure requirements for political advertising under the Honest Advertising Act, which is proposed by a bipartisan coalition of senators. The act would separate control over the solicitation and placement of ads from the separate functions of delivering and moderating content.

Lastly, the conventional media must be more forceful in debunking lies. Journalists need to expose the lies for what they are: pernicious, knowing, and deliberate perversions of the truth. They need to call out lies as lies, not as claims that are "baseless," or "without evidence." Journalists should never succumb to the "false equivalency" or "both sides" approach to reporting that gives equal play to lies and truth.

# Corrupt Justice

## *Redeeming Law Enforcement*

> Man's capacity for justice makes democracy possible, but
> man's inclination to injustice makes democracy necessary.
>
> —Theologian and political philosopher
> Reinhold Niebuhr, 1944

The mission statement that the United States Department of Justice emblazons on its website pledges "fair and impartial administration of justice for all Americans." It quotes Thomas Jefferson's reminder that "the most sacred of the duties of government [is] to do equal and impartial justice to all its citizens." It affirms that "this sacred duty remains the guiding principle for the women and men of the U.S. Department of Justice."

The president's unchecked constitutional power to pardon anyone for federal crimes presents the sternest test of impartial justice for the exalted and the humble. President Bill Clinton, on his final day as president, seemed to violate this principle by pardoning the billionaire fugitive Marc Rich. In 1983, federal prosecutors led by then U.S. Attorney Rudy Giuliani, indicted Rich on sixty-five counts of tax evasion, racketeering, and breaking the oil embargo to trade with Iran while it held American citizens hostage. Rich's charged crimes—which added up to a potential sentence of three hundred years—landed him on the FBI's most wanted list when he escaped trial by fleeing to Switzerland. His former wife, Denise Rich, had contributed to Hillary Clinton's New York Senate campaign and Bill Clinton's Presidential Library Fund.

The Rich pardon brought swift condemnation, not only from Republicans. Former Democratic President Jimmy Carter termed the pardon "disgraceful." The *New York Times* condemned it as "a shocking abuse of presidential power," and Democratic Representative Barney Frank of Massachusetts called it a "real betrayal" of Clinton's supporters. Although it was final, federal prosecutors and the U.S. House still investigated the pardon for possible bribery and obstruction of justice. The Justice Department, under President George W. Bush, closed the criminal case with no charges. However, the Republican-controlled House Government Reform Committee blasted Clinton for issuing a corrupt pardon that violated Justice Department guidelines. "President Clinton has sent the message that he had two standards of justice," the report said, "one for the rich, and one for the poor." A minority report by most Committee Democrats condemned the pardon "as indisputably a case of bad judgment." But it insisted that the Committee's record "does not support the allegation that President Clinton or any other Administration official was bribed or otherwise corrupted."

The Framers advisedly granted the president this unfettered power of grace as a last resort to rectify miscarriages of justice, show mercy where it is needed, and advance the public good. Alexander Hamilton wrote that "the criminal code of every country partakes so much of necessary severity, that without an easy access to exceptions in favor of unfortunate guilt, justice would wear a countenance too sanguinary and cruel." The president, he said, would dispense "the mercy of government," and when needed, "restore the tranquility of the commonwealth." The Rich pardon was not the first one to violate this intent.

In 1830, a federal judge sentenced George Wilson and James Porter to death for robbing the mails and endangering the life of a driver. Porter was hanged, but Wilson had influential friends in the administration of President Andrew Jackson. They talked Jackson into pardoning Wilson for these crimes. The pardon would spare him the noose but would leave his twenty-year sentence untouched for other crimes. The president "allowed himself to be influenced in an improper manner, to interfere with the legal course of justice," charged a *Baltimore Patriot* editorial. He removed "a confessedly guilty person from under its penalties, without sufficient mitigating circumstances—and suffered the great mass of citizens to feel that equal degrees of guilt do not lead to equal punishment." Yet, Wilson refused the pardon and chose death. The U.S. Supreme Court upheld his right to do so. Chief Justice John Marshall ruled that "a pardon is an act of grace, proceeding from the power entrusted with the execution of the laws." However, "delivery is not completed without acceptance."

President Andrew Johnson was an apostate Democrat who assumed the incumbency of the assassinated Republican President Abraham Lincoln. He opposed efforts to reconstruct the nation and integrate newly liberated slaves into American life. Johnson outraged congressional Republicans when he pardoned from the consequences of rebellion many thousands of wealthy, former Confederate planters, some of whom with their wives had wined and dined him in Washington. Johnson's pardons restored political and economic power to much of the old slaveholding elite, who proceeded to keep their former slaves poor, controlled, and powerless.

In 1967, Jimmy Hoffa, the corrupt president of the International Brotherhood of Teamsters, began serving a thirteen-year prison term for jury tampering, attempted bribery, conspiracy, and fraud. In anticipation of his 1972 reelection campaign, President Richard Nixon told his aides, we "can't exclude anyone," especially Teamsters, America's largest union, and "hard hat" construction workers who backed the war and Middle American values. On December 23, 1971, Nixon commuted Hoffa's remaining sentence, subject to his abstention from union leadership. Upon his release, Hoffa received $1.75 million in retirement benefits from the Teamsters. In 1972, the union departed from its customary practice of supporting Democrats and endorsed Nixon. On July 30, 1975, Hoffa vanished from in front of a restaurant near Detroit. He was declared dead in 1982, but the whereabouts of his body remains a notorious mystery.

Following President Nixon's resignation, his appointed vice president, Gerald Ford, became president, although he had never been elected to a position higher than that of a congressman from Grand Rapids, Michigan. In his most notable decision, President Ford granted a complete and unconditional pardon to Nixon for any crimes he might have committed against the United States. "Our long national nightmare is over," he said. Ford was wrong. The nightmare of Watergate lives on in America's collective memory, and Nixon escaped full accountability for his crimes. However, most historians now agree that without this pardon, Ford's presidency might well have been consumed by Nixon's prosecutions and trials.

In the 1890s, Congress established an Office of the Pardon Attorney within the Department of Justice to ensure the scrupulous and just granting of pardons. Convicted offenders may apply for a pardon from that office. They must wait five years after the federal conviction, submit three character references, and undergo a rigorous investigation. Petitioners "should bear in mind that a presidential pardon is ordinarily a sign of forgiveness" and must consider "the petitioner's acceptance of responsibility, remorse, and atonement for the offense." A pardon "is not a sign of vindication and does not connote or establish innocence."

President Trump has left about fourteen thousand Pardon Office applicants languishing in limbo, while topping many times over the corruption of the Rich pardon. In August 2017, Trump foreshadowed his later rash of crony pardons, with his first pardon to a political ally, Arizona sheriff Joe Arpaio. A federal judge had charged Arpaio with criminal contempt for disobeying a court order to cease violating the constitutional rights of Hispanics, by targeting and detaining suspected undocumented immigrants through racial profiling. Trump pardoned Arpaio, before the judge sentenced him, and without Pardon Office review. Trump undermined an essential power of the courts for holding wrongdoers to account. No other president has fully pardoned anyone for criminal contempt prior to sentencing.

In his zeal to erase any trace of the investigation by Special Counsel Robert Mueller, the lame duck Trump pardoned former campaign associates that Mueller's team had prosecuted. Former campaign surrogate and National Security Advisor Michael Flynn had twice pleaded guilty to lying to the FBI about his conversations with the Russian ambassador. A jury had found former campaign chair Paul Manafort guilty of bank and tax fraud, illegal foreign lobbying, and witness tampering conspiracies. Another jury had convicted former political advisor Roger Stone of obstructing Congress, lying, and witness tampering. Former foreign policy advisor George Papadopoulos had pleaded guilty to lying to the FBI about his contacts with Russian agents. Unlike deputy campaign manager Rick Gates and attorney Michael Cohen, who cooperated truthfully with prosecutors and received no pardons, these figures had protected Trump with their silence and lies. Mueller's lead prosecutor, Andrew Weissmann, said that the team knew "we have the dangling of pardons to Stone and Manafort." Even Nixon had not dared to pardon cronies who had incriminating information about his Watergate scandal.

Trump preemptively pardoned his former campaign manager and White House chief strategist Steve Bannon. He had not yet stood trial for charges that he stole more than a million dollars from donations by Trump loyalists to a fund supposedly dedicated "100 percent" to building Trump's border wall. Although Bannon's conservative credentials had brought in the donors, his partners, who lacked the connections for a Trump pardon, remained vulnerable to imprisonment. Trump pardoned Elliot Broidy, one of Trump's leading fund raisers and vice chair of his inaugural committee. Broidy had pleaded guilty to illegally lobbying the Trump administration to abandon one of the government's largest fraud and money laundering cases against a Malaysian billionaire. He also had illegally lobbied the administration to deport to China a critic of the Communist regime. Broidy admitted paying $1.6 million to silence a woman with whom he had an extramarital affair involving a pregnancy and abortion.

Trump pardoned a slew of corrupt former officials. He pardoned former Republican Congressman Randall "Duke" Cunningham, who served eight years in prison for accepting some $2.4 million from defense contractors in cash bribes, rent-free living on a yacht, and payments for prostitutes, travel, and jewelry. "This SOB literally sold out America for cash, betraying his oath and our country," said Jon Fleischman, the former executive director of the California Republican Party. "He didn't deserve a pardon." Retired reporter Onell Soto, who won a Pulitzer Prize as part of the team that broke Cunningham's scandal, called him the "most corrupt congressman ever caught." Trump's ally, the former Republican speaker of the U.S. House Newt Gingrich, who had abetted Cunningham's corruption by putting him on the Defense Appropriations Subcommittee, strenuously advocated for the pardon.

Trump pardoned former Republican Representative Chris Collins, who had pleaded guilty to insider stock trading and lying to federal investigators. He pardoned former Republican Representative Duncan Hunter, who had pleaded guilty to diverting campaign funds to pay for luxury hotels, posh vacations to Italy and Hawaii, private school tuition for his children, and "personal relationships" with several women. Collins and Hunter were the first members of Congress to endorse Trump's 2016 campaign for president.

On December 22, 2020, Trump granted the most notorious pardons in U.S. history. He pardoned four employees of the private security firm Blackwater who were convicted in 2014 of murder and manslaughter in the mass killing of fourteen unarmed, innocent men, women, and two boys, aged nine and eleven. A federal court found that in 2007, without provocation, the Blackwater guards had opened fire on civilians in Baghdad's Nisour Square with machine guns and grenade launchers. "We had never done anything like this before," said Ronald C. Machen, the U.S. Attorney who supervised the case. "We had to send teams of FBI agents and prosecutors over there to build the case from the ground up—they had to risk their lives to collect evidence. We had to persuade Iraqis who lost loved ones to come over to testify. . . . And to think it all gets thrown away." Haider Ahmed Rabia, who was one of more than thirty survivors who testified and who still lives with bullets in his legs, said, "Today they proved to me it was just theater."

The pardons repudiated the rule of law by a professed "right to life" and "law and order" president. "With those sentences reversed by the stroke of a pen, who will trust the American justice system again?" said Sarah Holewinski, Washington director at Human Rights Watch. The *Washington Post* editorialized that "the fact that he did not pardon a fifth Blackwater guard who cooperated with prosecutors underlined his contempt for the rule of law." The head of Blackwater then was Trump ally Erik Prince, who is also the brother of Trump's Education Secretary, Betsy DeVos. Not coincidentally, Joe Biden, who was vice president at the time, had pushed for prosecutions of the Blackwater guards.

Perhaps naïvely, America's founders had anticipated that presidents would use the awesome pardon power circumspectly. Hamilton assured critics that "the reflection that the fate of a fellow-creature depended on his sole fiat, would naturally inspire scrupulousness and caution." But Framer George Mason had warned of a self-serving president like Donald Trump, who "may frequently pardon crimes which were advised by himself. It may happen, at some future day, that he will establish a monarchy, and destroy the republic." James Madison agreed but pointed to the deterrent of impeachment: "There is one security in this case to which gentlemen may not have adverted: if the President be connected, in any suspicious manner, with any person, and there be grounds to believe he will shelter him, the House of Representatives can impeach him: they can remove him if found guilty."

Even before pardoning Arpaio in August 2017, Trump had begun politicizing justice. He was not the first president to do so. Under pressure from President George W. Bush, his attorney general had fired, in the middle of his second term, nine U.S. Attorneys, not for cause, but because they did not sufficiently pursue the false allegations of voter fraud by Democrats. Political appointees in Bush's Department of Justice illegally applied political criteria to the hiring of civil service employees. The White House obstructed Congress's investigation of these scandals by destroying messages unlawfully sent and received on private servers and by withholding documents and witnesses. A report by the inspector general for the Department of Justice found that Attorney General Alberto Gonzales had caved to political pressure from above and "abdicated his responsibility to safeguard the integrity and independence of the department." Gonzales resigned in August 2007.

Trump's corruption of Justice surpassed the misdeeds of every previous president. Within a week of his inauguration, Trump toppled the barrier that traditionally protects the Department of Justice from White House pressure. In private, on January 27, 2017, Trump asked FBI Director James Comey to pledge personal loyalty to the president. Less than a month later, Trump asked Comey to end the investigation of Michael Flynn, saying, "I hope you can let this go." Trump did not intervene out of compassion for Flynn, who had lied to the FBI and secretly taken money to lobby for Turkey. Trump worried that Flynn would negotiate a deal with investigators and disclose what he knew about his campaign's collusion with the Russians.

Trump continued to interfere with the Flynn case. In November 2017, Trump's personal counsel John Dowd told Flynn's lawyer on a voicemail that "it wouldn't surprise me if you've gone on to make a deal with . . . the government. . . . [I]f . . . there's information that implicates the president, then we've got a national security issue . . . so, you know . . . we need some kind of heads-up." The message, wrote Special Counsel Robert Mueller, "could have affected both (Flynn's) willingness to cooperate and the completeness of that cooperation." It is not credible that Dowd would have delivered this message without approval from his client, the president.

After replacing his lawyers with counsel recommended by Trump associates, Flynn petitioned to withdraw his guilty plea and ceased his cooperation with the government, which had gone poorly anyway. The presiding federal judge, Emmet G. Sullivan, rejected charges of FBI and prosecutorial misconduct from Flynn's new attorneys. He refused to let Flynn renege on his twice-pled admission of guilt. Trump then called for Justice to drop the charges against Flynn; Attorney General William Barr complied. The lead prosecutor, Brandon L. Van Grack, withdrew in protest, and only Trump loyalist and political appointee Justice Timothy Shea signed on.

Former Justice prosecutor Jonathan Kravis charged that Trump and Barr had "undercut the work of career employees to protect an ally of the president, an abdication of the commitment to equal justice under the law." He said, Barr has sent "an unmistakable message to prosecutors and agents—if the president demands, we will throw you under the bus." Kravis resigned from the Department of Justice. "I resigned from the Justice Department after ten years as a career prosecutor," he said. "I left a job I loved," because I "was not willing to serve a department that would so easily abdicate its responsibility to dispense impartial justice."

Of more than one hundred thousand prosecutions initiated by the Department of Justice during Barr's tenure, he only intervened in order to drop prosecution after a guilty plea in the Flynn case. Former federal prosecutors could not recall any similar intervention. Although Trump's pardon of Flynn mooted the case, Judge Sullivan advisedly noted that "President Trump's decision to pardon Mr. Flynn is a political decision, not a legal one. . . . However, the pardon does not, standing alone, render [Flynn] innocent of the alleged violation."

Trump had appointed Barr to replace former Alabama Republican Senator Jeff Sessions, a campaign surrogate, who had infuriated the president by recusing himself from matters related to the 2016 elections. The president had expected Sessions to become his fixer in the mold of former personal lawyers Michael Cohen and earlier Roy Cohn, the notorious Senator Joseph McCarthy's former aide. "The only reason I gave him the job," Trump said, "was because I felt loyalty. He was an original supporter." However, Sessions left Trump disappointed. "Where's my Roy Cohn?" Trump asked. Like Cohn and Cohen, Trump had expected Sessions to facilitate and cover up Trump's misdeeds and punish his enemies. Cohen explained to Congress that "being Trump's 'fixer' was my job. It was always about to stay on message. Always defend. It monopolized my life." Cohen explained that "if somebody does something Mr. Trump doesn't like, I do everything in my power to resolve it to Mr. Trump's benefit."

Sessions resisted presidential pressure until he resigned on November 7, 2018. Trump then found his reincarnated Roy Cohn in William Barr, who won Senate confirmation on February 14, 2019. Trump reaped immediate political dividends from his new fixer when Barr defused the report that Special Counsel Robert Mueller completed in March 2019. Prior to the report's public release the following month, Barr discounted its findings in a written summary and a press conference. In response, the usually diffident Mueller wrote that Barr "did not fully capture the context, nature, and substance" of his report. "There is now public confusion about critical aspects of the results of our investigation."

As Trump's political appointee, Barr should have steered clear of Mueller's investigation. But he exonerated Trump from obstruction of justice, although the report documented ten cases of interference with the Mueller investigation. More than six hundred federal prosecutors, who had worked under Republican and Democratic presidents, said that Mueller's findings justified "multiple felony charges for obstruction of justice. . . . [T]he evidence of corrupt intent and connection to pending proceedings is overwhelming."

The tradition of independent special prosecutors or counsels began with probes into the scandals of the so-called Great Barbecue—the corruption of government for personal gain during the administration of President Ulysses Grant in the 1870s. Without political independence, Congress and the public cannot trust their conclusions. That independence has inevitably led to clashes with presidents. Trump was not the first president to interfere with a special prosecutor's investigation or attempt to derail the investigation altogether.

The Grant scandals implicated several of his closest allies, including Secretary of War William Belknap and private secretary Orville E. Babcock. In 1875, under pressure to ensure an unbiased inquiry, Grant appointed former Senator John B. Henderson as the nation's first special prosecutor. Politics immediately got in the way. The Republican press vilified Henderson as hostile to the president, and Grant's confidants murmured the same thought in his ear. So, the president meddled in the investigation. He decided that no witness should be granted immunity, which hobbled the prosecutions. Grant fired Henderson for indicting Babcock. The president replaced him with attorney James Broadhead, who had little time to prepare for complex cases. Grant gave an exculpatory deposition in the Babcock trial, which likely swayed the jury to acquit his corrupt aide. No other sitting president before or since has testified in a criminal trial. Grant's interference with investigation of the scandals tarnished his legacy as president.

When the Watergate investigation touched upon President Richard Nixon, Democrats and some Republicans in Congress demanded that he appoint a special prosecutor. Nixon resisted, but the Democrats who controlled the Senate made it a condition for approval of Nixon's nominee, Eliot Richardson, to fill the vacant position of attorney general. Richardson appointed Harvard professor and former solicitor general under presidents Kennedy and Johnson, Archibald Cox, as the Watergate special prosecutor. The appointment infuriated Nixon. "If Richardson searched specifically for the man whom I least trusted, he could hardly have done better," Nixon privately said.

Cox subpoenaed the tapes that Nixon had secretly recorded of presidential conversations. When Cox rejected Nixon's order to cease issuing subpoenas, the president fired him in what became known as the Saturday Night Massacre. On Saturday night, October 20, 1973, Nixon ordered Richardson to dismiss Cox. Richardson refused and resigned. He then ordered Deputy Attorney General William Ruckelshaus to carry out the firing. Ruckelshaus likewise refused and resigned. Finally, Solicitor General Robert Bork fired Cox, became the acting attorney general, and announced that his department had abolished the Office of Special Prosecutor. Bork would later pay a steep price for this acquiescence. In 1987, the Senate rejected President Ronald Reagan's appointment of Bork to the U.S. Supreme Court. Under pressure, Nixon ordered the compliant Bork to replace Cox with Leon Jaworski—a former "Democrat for Nixon"—whom the president thought would downplay the investigation. To Nixon's chagrin, Jaworski continued to investigate the Watergate scandal fully and faithfully.

The tipping point in the Watergate scandal was not the release of the White House tapes in 1974, but the Saturday Night Massacre. Nixon's attempted cover-up precipitated a fierce backlash from the public and from members of both parties in Congress. It set off the chain of events that led Nixon to avoid impeachment and conviction by resigning the presidency. Nixon's personal lawyer Leonard Garment said that after the firing, the president "thought of little else except to marvel 'over the mischief we had wrought and the public relations disaster we had brought on ourselves.'" On November 14, 1973, federal district court judge Gerhard Gesell ruled that in arbitrarily sacking Cox, Nixon had illegally violated the Justice Department's regulation that required "good cause" for firing a special prosecutor. "The discharge of Mr. Cox," Gesell said, "precipitated a widespread concern, if not lack of confidence, in the administration of justice." Gesell's decision was moot. Jaworski was already in place, and Cox disdained any attempt to reclaim his position.

Trump and Barr again undermined Special Counsel Mueller by meddling in the criminal sentencing of Roger Stone. The four career Justice prosecutors in the Stone case deemed his seven felonies sufficiently heinous to recommend seven to nine years in prison. This was at the upper end of federal sentencing guidelines. Trump tweeted back, "this is a horrible and very unfair situation. The real crimes were on the other side, as nothing happens to them. Cannot allow this miscarriage of justice!"

Barr obliged Trump at the eleventh hour in February 2020. He circumvented professional prosecutors to recommend a much lighter sentence for Stone. Barr disingenuously denied any influence from Trump, but the four career prosecutors withdrew from the case. Again, Timothy Shea, who played no part in the prosecution, unilaterally signed the new sentencing memo. The National Association of Assistant U.S. Attorneys objected that "recommendations on sentencing should be developed by the career prosecutors" and "should be made impartially and without the political influence of elected officials." More than two thousand former prosecutors from both Republican and Democratic administrations demanded Barr's resignation. His intervention for Stone, they said, "openly and repeatedly flouted" the Department's "sacred obligation to ensure equal justice under the law."

Aaron Zelinsky, one of Stone's prosecutors, testified before Congress that Stone was "being treated differently from any other defendant because of his relationship to the president." He added, "What I saw was the Department of Justice exerting significant pressure on the line prosecutors in the case to obscure the correct Sentencing Guidelines calculation to which Roger Stone was subject—and to water down and in some cases outright distort the events that transpired in his trial and the criminal conduct that gave rise to his conviction." As an employee of an office under Barr's supervision, Zelinsky had testified against his personal interest in an administration known for its harsh retaliation against critics. Stone avoided any prison time for his crimes when Trump commuted his sentence in July 2020 and followed up with a full pardon.

In June 2020, Barr and Trump used lies, cajolery, and intimidation to fire Geoffrey Berman, the U.S. Attorney for the Southern District of New York. Although Trump had appointed Berman, this district has a history of independence and Berman was reportedly leading Trump-related investigations. Berman testified before the House Judiciary Committee that "the Attorney General said that if I did not resign from my position, I would be fired. . . . I told him that while I did not want to get fired, I would not resign." Berman testified that his removal would lead to a "disruption" and "delay" of ongoing investigations, which Barr and Trump apparently hoped for. Berman testified that Barr, in effect, had tried to bribe him into resigning by offering him other positions. Barr told the press that Berman was "stepping down," even though he knew that Berman had no intention of doing so. When Berman exposed the lie, President Trump fired him. Neither Barr nor Trump gave a reason for the sack, which Berman testified was "unprecedented, unnecessary, and unexplained."

Berman's firing followed Barr's removal of Jessie Liu, the former U.S. Attorney for the District of Columbia, who was investigating Trump associates. Trump promised to appoint Liu to the post of Under Secretary for the Office of Terrorist Financing and Financial Crimes. But she withdrew her nomination because of doubts from Republicans about her conservative credentials and loyalty to the president. Barr replaced her with Trump crony Timothy Shea. Paul Rosenzweig, the former deputy assistant secretary for policy in the Department of Homeland Security, wrote, "this is how an authoritarian works to subvert justice. He purports to uphold the forms of justice . . . while undermining the substance of justice."

Trump, with Barr's compliance, became the first president to investigate criminally his defeated opponent. In 2018, after Trump had relentlessly attacked "Crooked Hillary Clinton," the Justice Department launched yet another investigation of the Clinton Foundation and her use of a private email server. The investigation dragged on for almost two years, until January 2020, when it ended with no findings of wrongdoing.

Without a clear predicate, Trump's Justice Department secretly subponeaed the private records of two of Trump's "avowed" enemies in Congress, Democrats Adam B. Schiff and Eric Swalwell. They further collected data on staff and family members. The Department also seized in secret the phone records of journalists who worked for media companies that Trump had repeatedly bashed: the *New York Times*, the *Washington Post*, and CNN. As in the Clinton case, none of these investigations led to any findings of wrongdoing. John Dean, Richard Nixon's White House Counsel, who became a key Watergate witness, said these violations are "beyond Nixon." They are Nixon on "stilts and steroids."

John W. Elias, a career attorney who held senior positions in the Antitrust Division of Trump's Justice Department, disclosed political interference by Trump and Barr in civil litigation. On August 21, 2019, Trump attacked California's tough rules on automobile emissions. A day later, Elias said that without a staff finding or full review of the case, Justice's political leadership began to probe California's rules. The investigation had little basis in law and "did not appear to be in good faith," Elias said. Still, political appointees moved forward, until Justice shuttered the investigation in February 2020. In 2017, after Trump complained about CNN, Justice sued to block AT&T's acquisition of Time Warner, CNN's parent company. The courts sided with AT&T.

In 2019, author E. Jean Carroll charged in an article for the *New Yorker* that Trump had raped her in the 1990s. When Trump accused her of lying, Carroll sued him for defamation. She said, like Monica Lewinsky in the Bill Clinton scandal, that she had DNA evidence for the rape. She asked the court to order President Trump to provide a DNA sample, as Clinton had done. After the court rejected Trump's motion to dismiss the lawsuit, his Justice Department intervened. It moved for the government to take charge of the case and remove Trump as a defendant, which would free him of liability. Justice attorneys claimed that Trump had acted in his official capacity as president when he accused Carroll of lying. The judge rejected this argument, denied Justice's motion in November 2020, and ordered the case to move forward.

Even Attorney General Barr, however, could not follow the president through the looking glass and endorse his fantasy that Democrats had robbed him of victory in 2020. Four weeks after Election Day, Barr contradicted Trump by affirming that "to date, we have not seen fraud on a scale that could have effected a different outcome in the election." Barr later announced his resignation, effective December 23, 2020. He resigned in time to avoid any complicity in Trump's incitement of the January 6 attack on the Capitol.

Every dictator in the modern world has bent the justice system to his will. Countries moving from democracy to autocracy today are suffering from politicized justice, which is a warning to the United States. Trump tested the independence of our Justice Department as it has never been tested before, and it proved far too vulnerable to presidential and political manipulation. Changes need to be made immediately to prevent further abuse.

## THE FIX: REFORM PARDONING, EXPAND DISCLOSURE, AND ERECT A FIREWALL BETWEEN THE WHITE HOUSE AND THE JUSTICE DEPARTMENT

Without infringing on the president's constitutional authority, Congress can still do much to restore fairness and impartiality to the federal system of justice. Congress cannot stop the president from granting pardons, but it should criminalize the exchange of a pardon for anything of value. It should set clear guidelines for pardons and require presidents to document any pardons linked to investigations of themselves or their family members. Presidential self-pardons should be explicitly prohibited, and the statute of limitations on crimes committed by a president should be waived to avoid immunity after leaving office.

Congress should require the Justice Department to make public the secret opinions of the Office of Legal Counsel. It should specify prohibited contacts between Justice Department officials and the White House and require the White House to maintain a registry of contacts for the House and Senate judiciary committees. The new law should include within the Department of Justice a confidential, non-retaliatory whistleblower line so that employees can report any suspected unethical or illegal conduct. Employees should be rewarded for complaints that prove wrongdoing.

Congress should enact legislation that would bar the president and White House officials from requesting or demanding any action by Justice officials regarding investigations, prosecutions or charging decisions of U.S. citizens. Exceptions would only apply in cases involving critical executive functions such as defending the nation's security. Such prohibitions are not unconstitutional; similar strictures apply to the Internal Revenue Service. An independent task force should propose means for ensuring fairness and impartiality in decisions on arrest, charging, prosecution, and sentencing decisions.

# · 6 ·

# Enemies of the People

## *Protecting a Free Press*

Whenever any hindrance, no matter what its name, is placed in the way of this information, a democracy is weakened, and its future endangered. This is the meaning of freedom of the press. It is not just important to democracy. It is democracy.

—Journalist Walter Cronkite, 1971

*N*o American president has suffered greater vilification from the press than now revered Abraham Lincoln. The press defamed him as a Filthy Storyteller, Despot, Liar, Thief, Braggart, Yahoo, Buffoon, Monster, Ignoramus, Scoundrel, Perjurer, Robber, Swindler, Tyrant, Fiend, Butcher, Ape, Demon, Beast, Baboon, Gorilla, Imbecile, and "the laughingstock of the whole world." The president refused to respond in kind. "If I were to read, much less answer, all the attacks made on me, this shop might as well be closed for any other business," he said. "If the end brings me out all right, what's said against me won't amount to anything. If the end brings me out wrong, ten angels swearing I was right wouldn't make any difference."

Lincoln was not indifferent to personal criticism, but rather than lashing back, he "cultivated, persuaded, shaped, and molded," malleable opinion makers, noted his biographer Allen C. Guelzo. Unlike Lincoln, President Donald Trump fiercely countered alleged press insults, criticisms, or the absence of glorified coverage. For Trump, who identified himself with the national will, the press was not solely his enemy. It was the "enemy of the people."

The Framers understood how a free press protects America's democracy. "To be governed by reason and truth," Thomas Jefferson wrote, "our first object should therefore be, to leave open to him all the avenues to truth. The most effectual hitherto found, is the freedom of the press. It is, therefore, the first shut up by those who fear the investigation of their actions."

"The freedom of the press is one of the greatest bulwarks of liberty, and can never be restrained but by despotic governments," affirmed George Mason in the Virginia Declaration of Rights. Madison singled out freedom of the press for primacy in his original version of what became a more abbreviated First Amendment: "The people shall not be deprived or abridged of their right to speak, to write, or to publish their sentiments; and the freedom of the press, as one of the great bulwarks of liberty, shall be inviolable."

Despite this high ideal, the American media have long endured challenges to their freedom, culminating in Trump's war against the press. President George Washington complained to a correspondent in 1793 of "diabolical" press calumnies, and "arrows of malevolence" that were "outrages on common decency." But Washington kept his grievances private and contemplated no official action against the press. "It is difficult to prescribe bounds to their effect," he said.

Washington's successor, fellow Federalist John Adams, had no such scruples. In 1798, the Federalist Congress passed, and John Adams signed, the Sedition Act, which made it a criminal offense to "write, print, utter or publish" false statements critical of Congress or the president. The act enshrined into law the Federalist view of an inviolate government that, once elected, should be immune to public clamor. "Liberty of the press and of opinion is calculated to destroy all confidence between man and man," wrote Federalist Representative John Allen of Connecticut. "It leads to the dissolution of every bond of union." Jefferson responded that self-serving Federalists were keeping the principles of his Democratic-Republican Party from "the public mind," which would triumph "if the knolege (sic) of facts can only be disseminated among the people."

This unpopular measure contributed to Jefferson's defeat of Adams in 1800 and the election of a pro-Jefferson Congress. Congress let the Sedition Act expire in 1801. "The firmness with which the people have withstood the late abuses of the press, the discernment they have manifested between truth and falsehood, show that they may safely be trusted to hear everything true and false, & to form a correct judgment between them," Jefferson wrote.

During the Civil War, President Lincoln focused on managing the content and flow of wartime news. While he tolerated personal attacks, Lincoln did not stand for press content that he believed compromised the war effort or threatened northern unity. Lincoln abandoned all restraint in the so-called bogus proclamation episode. In May 1864, two of the nation's leading opposition newspapers, the *New York World* and the *New York Journal of Commerce*, inadvertently published a forged presidential proclamation that seemed to call into question a Union victory in the still unsettled war. Disregarding claims that a fraudster had victimized the newspapers, President Lincoln ordered General John Adams Dix in New York to arrest and imprison the papers' editors, proprietors, and publishers, and seize their printing presses.

Secretary of War Edwin Stanton brushed off Dix's protests and wrote, "How you can excuse or justify delay in executing the President's order is not for me to determine." Local authorities soon apprehended the forger, and the administration cancelled its arrests and confiscations. Still, it had closed the two major newspapers for several days and sullied their reputations. The administration also took control of the Independent Telegraph Company for a time and shut down a news service run by independent journalist Henry Villard.

This episode reflected Lincoln's frustration in his efforts to control wartime communications in a time of rapid, decentralized technological change. As historian Menahem Blondheim explained, "the entire wartime system of public communications could be undermined. New, independent, and uncontrolled telegraph networks . . . had entered the field of real-time transmission. A competing wire service, not bound to the administration, had established itself as an alternative system for news gathering and diffusion."

To keep the press in line with his crusade to save democracy during the First World War, President Woodrow Wilson created a Committee on Public Information (CPI). With journalists restricted from wartime access to military leaders and administration officials, the CPI filled the gap with thousands of slanted, pro-government press releases. This overt propaganda sanitized news and manipulated facts to serve the administration. The CPI published its own official daily newspaper and distributed it to military installations, post offices, and other government facilities. "In some respects," said media historian Christopher B. Daly, the publication "is the closest the United States has come to a paper like the Soviet Union's *Pravda* or China's *People's Daily*." The committee even stooped to bribing journalists and subsidizing favorable news organizations.

To control the radical antiwar press, Wilson relied on repression under the wartime Espionage and Sedition acts. This legislation imposed stiff fines and imprisonment for publishing in broad terms, "disloyal, profane, scurrilous, or abusive language about the form of government of the United States." It authorized the postmaster general to close the mails to material that he deemed seditious. Postmaster General Albert Burleson denied mailing privileges to dozens of socialist and pacifist newspapers through war's end and beyond. Congress repealed the Sedition Act in December 1920, more than a year after the end of the war.

During the Great Depression of the 1930s and World War II, liberal anti-monopolists feared that large corporations would take control of print and broadcasting. They proposed regulating the press to ensure a diversity of opinion and prevent newspapers from controlling competitors in radio. Led by Elisha Hanson, general counsel for the American Newspaper Publishers Association, the press largely blunted regulatory efforts. "As long as we have a press free from government restraint in the performance of its function of gathering and disseminating information, whether in time of peace or war, their ideal will be preserved," Hanson said in 1939. The press, he said, must be "free from restrictive and poisonous government control."

The press faced stiff challenges from President Richard Nixon. "The press is your enemy," Nixon confided in February 1971 to Admiral Thomas H. Moorer, the chairman of the Joint Chiefs of Staff. He underscored: "Enemies. Understand that? . . . Now, never act that way . . . give them a drink, you know, treat them nice, you just love it, you're trying to be helpful. But don't help the bastards. Ever. Because they're trying to stick the knife right in our groin." Nixon kept his hard talk about the press private and worked his media strategy from behind the scenes. He relied on carefully arranged and choreographed speeches from Vice President Spiro Agnew to attack journalists as a "small and unelected elite" who possess "broad . . . powers of choice" and "decide what forty to fifty million Americans will learn of the day's events in the nation and the world." Without a warrant, Nixon secretly wiretapped journalists whom he found particularly troublesome and asked the IRS to investigate their tax returns.

Nixon's "real game plan," for the press, wrote political advisor Lyn Nofziger, is "making our own point in our own time and in our own ways that the press is liberal, pro-Democratic and biased." Still, more shrewdly than Trump, Nixon won media support through a combination of intimidation and cajolery. He won endorsements from 93 percent of the nation's daily newspapers for his reelection in 1972, compared to 12 percent for Donald Trump in 2020.

Shortly after taking office, President Ronald Reagan adopted a Reagan Doctrine to support anti-communist forces across the world, regardless of whether they respected democracy or human rights. The left-wing Sandinista government of Nicaragua was ground zero for the Reagan Doctrine. Administration officials financed a proxy war by the anti-Sandinista Contra guerilla army through subterranean channels after Congress banned the spending of funds directly or indirectly for military operations in Nicaragua. To drum up public support for the Contras, who were known for their atrocities against civilians, Reagan created a secret propaganda unit called the Office of Public Diplomacy (OPD).

The OPD worked to manipulate and control the media. It leaked classified and sometimes "unevaluated" information that reinforced the administration's position on Nicaragua. Its staff wrote opinion editorials for the *New York Times* deceptively submitted under the bylines of Contra leaders. The OPD's director for Latin America and the Caribbean, Otto Juan Reich, met dozens of times with major print and broadcast outlets. He cajoled and pressured them to follow the Reagan propaganda line on Nicaragua. The OPD secretly financed and aired negative television ads against members of Congress who did not support the president's policies. It misleadingly organized a media tour of Contra leaders through a "cut-out" to conceal its involvement. The operation planted a widely covered but bogus story that the Soviets were sending MIG fighter jets to the Sandinistas. A 1987 report by the U.S. Comptroller General Counsel Harry R. Van Cleve, a Reagan appointee, found that the OPD had "engaged in prohibited, covert propaganda activities designed to influence the media and the public to support the Administration's Latin America policies."

Donald Trump's campaign against the press was nasty, overt, and personal. He harangued journalists with a grab bag of gripes, grievances, slurs, and epithets. "I had a forty-five-year good relationship with the press, and what the hell happened?" Trump asked his New York friend Anthony Scaramucci, who served for eleven days as White House communications director. Scaramucci blamed the soured romance on Trump, not the media. "I told him, You declared war! You had Steve Bannon [Trump's White House strategist] declare war."

Bannon's strategy, like Nixon's, turned on discrediting the allegedly liberally biased "mainstream media." Bannon assured Trump that this ploy would insulate him from negative coverage and discredit any disclosures about his misdeeds. "I don't think it's good for democracy that we're branding an entire industry as an enemy," said Sean Spicer, Trump's first press secretary. "But is it effective? I think so."

In a chat with President Trump, shortly after his 2016 victory, with no cameras rolling, veteran CBS News correspondent Leslie Stahl later recalled that she queried Trump about his attack on the mainstream media as "fake news." Stahl asked, "You know, you've won, why do you keep hammering at this?" Trump responded, "You know why I do it? I do it to discredit you all and demean you all, so that when you write negative stories about me, no one will believe you."

The fake news that poisoned the 2016 presidential campaign did not come from CNN, the *New York Times*, or CBS News. It came from Russian intelligence operatives bolstered by fake news writers in the economically depressed city of Veles in Macedonia. This flash flood of fabricated news boosted Trump and disparaged the Clintons: "Pope Francis Shocks World, Endorses Donald Trump for President"; "FBI Agent Suspected in Hillary Email Leaks Found Dead in Apparent Murder-Suicide"; and "Bill Clinton Loses It in Interview—Admits He's a Murderer."

Although easy to dismiss, studies have shown that such outlandish stories matter. An estimated 25 percent of Americans visited a fake news site within a six-week period during the 2016 campaign. "The top 20 [provable] fake election news stories in 2016 generate more shares, reactions, and comments on Facebook than the top 20 election stories from all 19 major news outlets combined," an analysis by Buzzfeed News found. Another study by Ohio State University professors looked at voters who backed Obama in 2012. They found that controlling for other factors, Obama voters who believed one or more of three widely circulated fake news stories from 2016, were 3.3 times more likely to defect from the Democratic ticket than those who rejected these false claims.

Donald Trump formally declared war on the press at Trump Tower on January 11, 2017, during his first press conference as president-elect. Trump refused to answer a question from CNN senior White House correspondent Jim Acosta. "Your organization is terrible," he shouted at Acosta. "I am not going to give you a question. You are fake news." Acosta said that Trump's press secretary Sean Spicer threatened to toss him out of Trump Tower if he dared to ask another question. A month later, Trump tweeted, "The FAKE NEWS media (failing @nytimes @ NBCNews @ABC @CBS @CNN) is not my enemy, it is the enemy of the American people!" Trump had recycled an accusation used by Soviet dictator Joseph Stalin to silence his opposition, often by assassination or imprisonment in the Gulag network of concentration camps. Trump has publicly reiterated that accusation or its equivalent in more than 2,500 tweets and many public appearances.

Trump did not war against all media. He followed a dual strategy aimed at denigrating responsible journalism while promoting actual fake news. Responsible journalists sometimes make mistakes, but they admit their errors and continue striving to discover and report the truth. Fake news is manufactured by design. Trump loves and promotes tales invented by foreign sources or the American right that serve his interests. Deliberately, Trump has turned fake news into real journalism and real journalism into fake news.

Trump collided with Acosta again at a press conference on November 7, 2018. When Acosta asked about Trump's exploitation of race, Trump retorted, "you are a rude, terrible person. You shouldn't be working for CNN." The administration then suspended Acosta's press pass and access to the White House grounds. It claimed that during the conference, "he put his hands" on a White House intern. Video only showed that he had lightly brushed her arm when he lowered his arm to prevent her from taking his microphone. The next day, the White House circulated a doctored video from conspiracy theorist Paul Joseph Watson that compressed frames to make the contact appear more severe than it was. Federal District Court Judge Timothy Kelly, a Trump appointee, issued a temporary order restoring Acosta's White House credentials. The administration complied, and the case ended there.

In February 2019, Facebook banned Watson and other far-right conspiracy mongers "that promote or engage in violence and hate." It banned anti-Muslim extremist Laura Loomer, who said, "How many more people need to die before everyone agrees that Islam is cancer & we should never let another Muslim into the civilized world?" It banned Alex Jones, the leader of the InfoWars conspiracy website. He had infamously claimed that the 2012 massacre at Sandy Hook Elementary School was a "false flag" staged to embarrass gun rights activists, with "crisis actors" posing as dead children. Watson edited InfoWars and backed Jones's conspiracy theories. Trump rushed to defend Watson. He lamented the silencing of a "Conservative thinker," and slammed Facebook for censoring the other alleged conservative voices. "It's getting worse and worse for Conservatives on social media!" he tweeted. Trump has retweeted Watson a couple of times, but Donald Trump Jr. outpaced his father by retweeting Watson several dozens of times.

Trump-favored extremists like Watson and Jones are the faces of fake news, not mainstream professional journalists. Extremists violate every canon of responsible reporting to purvey toxic disinformation. They exploit tragedies, smear public figures, and play on bigotry and racism. Yet, Trump protects and praises them while assailing credible journalists with epithets never before heard from a president: "human scum," "animals," "crazy," "dumb," "nasty," and "some of the worst human beings you'll ever meet." Trump personally targeted women reporters, especially women of color, with insults like "loser," "very nasty," and "faker." He questioned their competence and their motives. Before the final presidential debate on October 22, 2020, Trump said that the African American moderator, NBC's Kristen Welker, has "always been terrible & unfair, just like most of the Fake News reporters."

Thinly veiled threats of violence underscored Trump's assault on the press. On July 2, 2017, Trump shared a doctored video, posted under the hashtag #FraudNewsCNN. It showed him slamming to the ground and repeatedly punching a person with a CNN logo superimposed on his head. A month later, Trump tweeted and then took down a meme of a "Trump train" crashing into someone with a CNN logo planted on their face. On Christmas Eve in 2017, Trump retweeted a concocted image of the CNN logo imposed on what appeared to be a bloodlike splatter under his shoe. During a "Make America Great" rally in Missoula, Montana, on October 18, 2018, Trump praised Representative Greg Gianforte for body slamming a reporter who had asked him a question about health care.

On October 26, 2018, federal authorities arrested ardent Trump supporter Cesar Sayoc Jr. He had sent pipe bombs to CNN, prominent Democrats, George Soros, and other perceived Trump critics. Hours later, at a campaign rally, Trump issued a passive voice denunciation of "political violence" to cries of "CNN Sucks!" He then turned his ire on the media, with the heated rhetoric that had inspired Sayoc. Unlike the tortured Raskolnikov of Dostoyevsky's *Crime and Punishment*, Trump never broods over the consequences of his acts. When asked if he took any responsibility for instilling hatred of the media, Trump replied, "not at all, no."

After a gunman killed five staff members at the offices of the *Capital Gazette* in Annapolis, Maryland, on June 28, 2018, Trump offered his "thoughts and prayers." However, with a thumbs up gesture, he swept past reporters asking him to address the massacre. Only the next evening, in scripted remarks, did Trump comment on the shooting and condemn violence against journalists. On the one-year anniversary of the Annapolis murders, at a meeting with Russian President Vladimir Putin in Osaka, Japan, Trump turned to Putin and said, "Get rid of them. Fake news is a great term, isn't it? You don't have this problem in Russia, but we do." Putin responded in English, "We also have. It's the same." They then "shared a chuckle."

During the protests that followed the killing by a Minneapolis police officer of George Floyd on May 25, 2020, the *New York Times* reported that "reporters and news photographers describe being roughed up, arrested and shot with projectiles while covering demonstrations across the country. . . . In interviews, reporters said they had identified themselves as members of the press before police fired projectiles, drew their weapons or pepper-sprayed them." By mid-June, the U.S. Press Freedom Tracker had reported 160 acts of violence by police against journalists, forty-nine arrests, and forty-two incidents of newsroom and equipment damage.

Trump said nothing about the arrest and harassment of journalists but blamed the media for violence. "The Lamestream Media is doing everything within their power to foment hatred and anarchy," Trump tweeted on May 31, 2020. "As long as everybody understands what they are doing, that they are FAKE NEWS and truly bad people with a sick agenda, we can easily work through them to GREATNESS." As the 2020 election approached, Trump became the first president to sue a media company—not just one, but three: the *New York Times*, the *Washington Post*, and CNN. The lawsuits targeted not "fake news" stories, but opinion pieces. Even at face value, these suits fell far short of the high bar set by the Supreme Court for defamation of a public figure. They had no traction in court, but they still sent out a warning to the press.

In April 2020, Trump's campaign shifted to a more vulnerable target. It sued a small local NBC station in the swing state of Wisconsin after it aired anti-Trump advertising by the Democratic super PAC, Priorities USA. The broadcast played Trump's words minimizing the COVID-19 threat, while showing a chart displaying the rising count of cases. The super PAC ran the ad in many stations across the nation, but the Trump campaign pursued only the Wisconsin outlet. The Reporter's Committee for the Freedom of the Press noted that Trump is "sending a clear message to news outlets: run an ad against me and risk an expensive lawsuit." Trump dropped the lawsuit after he lost the 2020 election.

Trump threatened to raise postal rates for shipments by Amazon, which is owned by Jeff Bezos, who also owns the *Washington Post* through a separate company. Trump said that he was scrutinizing a competition between Amazon and Microsoft for a $10 billion Defense Department contract. When Microsoft won the contract, Amazon filed suit. It alleged that Trump launched "behind-the-scenes attacks" against the company, which cost it the contract despite "clear failures" in Microsoft's proposal. In February 2020, Court of Claims Judge Patricia Campbell-Smith issued under seal a temporary injunction to halt work on the contract. She ruled that Amazon was likely to succeed in its complaint.

In May 2020, after Twitter put fact-check warnings on two of Trump's misleading tweets, he signed an executive order to limit the liability protection for private online platforms like Twitter and Facebook. Likely realizing that the order had no teeth, Trump demanded—without success—that Congress include in its 2020 defense appropriation an unrelated rider to repeal Section 230 of the 1996 Communications Decency Act. It shields social media companies from liability for content on their platforms. Congress refused to go along.

For Trump, the media further harms the people by propagating false alarms. When the COVID-19 outbreak began spreading in the United States in February 2020, Trump accused the media of reporting too much, not too little. Trump tweeted that CNN and MSNBC "are doing everything possible to make the Caronavirus (sic) look as bad as possible, including panicking markets, if possible. . . . USA in great shape!" Two days later, he called reports about the epidemic "the new hoax." On October 27, he said at a rally, "With the fake news, everything is COVID, COVID, COVID, COVID." At the end of February 2020, the United States had fewer than one hundred cases and only two deaths. By the time Trump left office, the case load had approached twenty-five million and the death toll had surpassed four hundred thousand.

During his 2020 campaign, Trump pioneered a new form of intimidation by attacking the media for polling results that he found unsatisfactory. On June 10, 2020, after a CNN poll showed that Trump trailed Joe Biden by fourteen percentage points nationally, his campaign threatened legal action unless CNN retracted and apologized for the poll. "To my knowledge, this is the first time in its forty-year history that CNN has been threatened with legal action because an American politician or campaign did not like CNN's polling results," wrote David C. Vigilante, the network's general counsel. Such "legal threats," he said, typically "come from countries like Venezuela and other regimes where there is little or no respect for a free and independent press." Then on June 18, the Trump-friendly outlet Fox News released a poll showing Trump behind Biden by twelve points nationally. The president didn't threaten legal action, but tweeted that "Fox News is out with another of their phony polls, done by the same group of haters that got it even more wrong in 2016. Watch what happens in November. Fox is terrible!"

Trump's assault on the media has eroded press credibility among his followers. A 2019 Pew Research Center study found that "Democrats' trust in many of these outlets has remained stable or in some cases increased since 2014." However, distrust increased "among Republicans for 14 of the 20 news sources . . . with particularly notable increases in distrust of CNN, the *New York Times* and the *Washington Post*—three frequent targets of criticism for President Donald Trump." An August 2020 Knight/Gallup survey found that two-thirds of Republicans had an unfavorable view of the media, compared to just 20 percent of Democrats.

## THE FIX: USE LAWSUITS AND PUBLIC EDUCATION, AND ENACT LAWS TO PROTECT JOURNALISTS

The United States pioneered freedom of the press, but now it ranks only forty-fifth in the world for press freedom and protection of reporters and journalists. America's free press advocates should ironically keep in their arsenal Trump's favorite tactic of the lawsuit. PEN America, a proponent of literary freedom, pioneered this approach by filing a 2018 lawsuit to prevent the president from "using the machinery of government to retaliate or threaten reprisals against journalists and media outlets for coverage he dislikes." In March 2020, U.S. District Court Judge Lorna C. Schofield ruled that the lawsuit could proceed to discovery. She found that "Defendant's [Trump's] actions have plausibly chilled the White House press corps' speech, the questions they ask Defendant and the reporting they consequently are able to publish." In February 2021, PEN America and the Biden administration reached a settlement that upheld the group's standing to challenge a president's threats and acts of retaliation.

Supporters of a free press should intensify the campaign of public education that they began in 2019. Journalism groups and media organizations launched a new campaign called "Protect Press Freedom." They aired a one-minute television ad and reproduced it in print and digital form. The ad does not mention Trump by name but draws attention to situations in which press freedom is at risk.

Congress and the federal courts have failed to recognize protections of state laws that shield reporters from disclosing confidential sources to law enforcement. However, the media cannot act as an effective watchdog for the government without protecting its sources. The remedy is a federal "media shield" law, such as the Free Flow of Information Act. The House has enacted versions of this legislation, but so far, the bills have died in the Senate. New laws should also include an anti-SLAPP provision to safeguard the press from baseless, harassing lawsuits and prohibit the surveillance of journalists and any interference with members of the press doing their job.

SLAPP suits are intended to censor, intimidate, and silence vulnerable critics by burdening them with the cost of a protracted legal defense, like the suit that the Trump campaign filed against the local Wisconsin station company. An anti-SLAPP provision would not block lawsuits of substance but would deter lawsuits with the sole purpose of intimidation.

# • 7 •

# Profits Above Patriotism

## *Policing Conflicts of Interest*

An impairment of impartial judgment can occur in even
the most well-meaning men when their personal economic interests are affected by the business they transact
on behalf of the Government.

—United States Supreme Court, 1961

*In* 1778, Silas Deane, who represented the Continental Congress
in France, accepted a golden, bejeweled snuff box as a gift from King
Louis XVI. Deane proudly displayed the snuff box as a token of his diplomatic accomplishments. Critics charged that the gift was more likely
a source of his subservience to France. They said a government official
who received something of value from a foreign power crossed a line
separating the public interest from private gain. Arthur Lee, a delegate
to the Congress, who served with Deane as an envoy to France, said,
"Deane knew that it was one of the fundamental laws of our Union that
no person in the service of the United States should accept from any
king, prince, or minister any present or gratuity whatsoever . . . yet in
the face of this fundamental law, Mr. Deane accepted of a gold snuff,
set with diamonds, from the King of France."

Although the snuff box controversy faded amid the larger concerns
of war with England, the fears it stirred up did not. The nation's Framers worried that, like the Roman republic, their new republic could
implode from within through failings in the "moral habits of private
men in their public roles," as Edward Gibbon wrote in his well-studied
*The Decline and Fall of the Roman Empire.* Americans saw this corruption replayed in the British government. "Look at Britain," said patriot

orator Patrick Henry. "See there the bolts and bars of power: see the bribery and corruption defiling the fairest fabric that ever human nature reared!"

James Madison warned that America's head of state "might betray his trust to foreign powers" for private gain. He said that the executive "would not possess those great emoluments from his station, nor that permanent stake in the public interest which would place him out of the reach of foreign corruption: He would stand in need therefore *of being controlled* as well as supported." To guard against conflicts of interest from abroad, delegates to the Constitutional Convention of 1787 unanimously adopted the foreign Emoluments Clause, which stated, "No Title of Nobility shall be granted by the United States; And no Person holding any Office of Profit or Trust under them, shall, without the Consent of the Congress, accept of any present, Emolument, Office, or Title of any kind whatever, from any King, Prince, or foreign State." The prohibition is absolute; no amount is specified, and no quid pro quo from a foreign government, agent, or entity is required to trigger a violation. The Framers did not want to force Americans to guess whether private gain or the public good inspired presidential decisions.

Delegates wisely recognized that, without controls in the Constitution, and not in mutable statutes, the personal economic interests of an executive could compromise the national interest. The Emoluments Clause, writes Fordham Law Professor Zephyr Teachout, was no mere afterthought. It expressed "the animating spirit of the Constitutional Convention" that "goes to the heart of the fears at the Convention"— fears that have no less relevance today, more than two centuries later. Governor Edmund Randolph of Virginia, a delegate to the Constitutional Convention, said that the clause guarded against "the president receiving emoluments from foreign powers. If discovered, he may be impeached. . . . I consider, therefore, that he is restrained from receiving any present or emoluments whatever. It is impossible to guard better against corruption."

Despite dated language, the foreign Emoluments Clause endures as a timely restraint on human frailty and the corrupting power of private economic interests. In 1994, the Department of Justice's Office of Legal Counsel reaffirmed its urgent rationale: "Those who hold offices under the United States must give the government their unclouded judgment and their uncompromised loyalty. That judgment might be biased, and that loyalty divided, if they received financial benefits from a foreign government." The Counsel made it clear that "the language of the Emoluments Clause is both sweeping and unqualified." It covers not just foreign states, but all foreign governmental entities and agents, including government-controlled companies.

To guard against corruption from within, the Framers put a domestic emoluments clause in the Constitution, addressed to the president. It provides that "the President shall, at stated Times, receive for his Services, a Compensation, which shall neither be encreased [*sic*] nor diminished during the Period for which he shall have been elected, and he shall not receive within that Period any other Emolument from the United States, or any of them," for instance, state or local governments. This clause, too, is absolute. No amount is specified, and no fraudulent transaction is required to trigger a violation. Hamilton wrote that constitutional delegates sought to insulate the president from the potentially corrupting influence of Congress or state legislatures. With the president's salary fixed "once for all" each term, the legislature "can neither weaken his fortitude by operating on his necessities, nor corrupt his integrity by appealing to his avarice." Similarly, because "[n]either the Union, nor any of its members, will be at liberty to give . . . any other emolument," and the president will "have no pecuniary inducement to renounce or desert the independence intended for him by the Constitution."

In 1962, to limit conflicts of interest, Congress adopted strict ethical rules for federal employees. It generally prohibited executive branch officials and employees from participating in matters of financial interest to themselves or their immediate family members. The act did not clearly apply to the president or vice president. An influential report by the New York Bar Association concluded that these high officials "must inevitably be treated separately," given the discretion required to exercise presidential power.

In 1978, after Watergate, Congress enacted the Ethics in Government Act, which created the Office of Government Ethics and a public financial disclosure system. However, it did not explicitly apply conflict of interest rules to the president or the vice president. In 1989, Congress exempted these top officials from its coverage.

Nonetheless, despite the lack of a legal obligation, presidents have generally sought voluntarily to avoid conflicts of interest, although not without controversy. When Lyndon Johnson became president in 1963, critics questioned his ownership of broadcast outlets in Texas (in the name of his wife, Lady Bird). The Johnsons responded by turning the assets over to independent trustees with full management authority and no communication of business decisions with Lyndon or Lady Bird. In an oral history interview, trustee J. Waddy Bullion said that the president "did not want to have any connection with the business affairs of the Johnsons, and he wanted it to be run by his trustees." Jimmy Carter put his peanut farm and warehouse business into a similar trust when he assumed the presidency in 1977.

These trust arrangements have not fully addressed potential conflicts of interest for presidents. Johnson and Carter did not set up true "blind trusts." The presidents still owned the assets, which they had not liquidated, and knew that their decisions could affect the value and profits of the trust. Carter's successor, Ronald Reagan, adopted a more secure option, the true blind trust in which the president has knowledge neither of the assets included nor of the management. "When President Reagan took office, he liquidated all of his holdings and turned them over to a trusted financial professional," said Peter Bloom, a Washington, D.C., attorney. "And once he liquidated his holdings and placed them into a blind trust, he had no idea what assets were being held inside the trust." Thus, the four-step process includes divestiture of prior assets, creation of an independent trust to manage new assets, a "no peeking" rule for assets, and a wall of silence between the trustees and the president other than summary information for tax returns.

No president had ever entered the White House with as many potential conflicts of interest as Donald Trump. He controlled some five hundred businesses with far-flung interests around the world. However, Trump adopted a weaker trust arrangement than his predecessors. Like Johnson and Carter, Trump did not divest ownership of his assets, but supposedly relinquished all management responsibilities. However, he entrusted control to his sons, Eric and Donald Jr., not to independent administrators. There is less to this concession than meets the eye. Trump had already devolved decision-making authority to his children. In a deposition held two weeks before the 2016 election, Trump said, "I think as they've become older and wiser, I give them more and more decision-making ability. But—but they have the right to make a decision, yes."

Trump's arrangement does not satisfy any of the criteria for a secure blind trust. Trump retained ownership and licensing rights. He continued to profit personally from existing businesses, despite knowing how his decisions might affect their profitability. It is dubious whether he has refrained from ever talking business with his sons, and disturbingly, he did not pledge to separate himself from the many hundreds of partners in his enterprises. With his illiquid real estate assets and the need to settle his debts, Trump would have taken a massive financial hit from divestment. His attorney Sheri Dillon called it a "fire sale" that would destroy Trump's business empire. Maybe so. But no one forced Trump to run for the presidency, and he claimed a net worth of several billion dollars. He could lose much of his wealth and remain wealthy in retirement. The trade-off? Retaining the most important position in the world.

The publication of a president's tax returns offers further protection against conflicts of interest. Democratic Representative Anna G. Eshoo of California has introduced legislation for the compulsory publication of a president's tax returns. She explained that "only a full release of tax returns can provide the public with clear information as to potential conflicts of interest and whether there could be potential entanglements with foreign governments and foreign businesses." In 1973, when a congressional committee requested President Richard Nixon's tax returns from 1969 to 1972, he complied, despite an ongoing audit from the IRS. To his everlasting regret, Nixon loosely said that "people have got to know whether or not their president is a crook. Well, I am not a crook." Since then, until Trump, nearly every president has released tax returns, despite an automatic IRS audit of presidential returns. Gerald Ford was the one exception; he released ten years of summary data on his federal taxes.

Presidents submit financial disclosures under law, but the requirements lack specificity and detail. During the 2016 campaign, Trump said that he could not release his taxes because they were under audit, despite no such legal prohibition, the Nixon precedent, and decades of returns that were no longer under audit. He said he would release his returns when the audit was completed, but through the end of his term, Trump had failed to do so. A U.S. Supreme Court ruling in February 2021 provided New York State prosecutors with access to Trump's tax returns and other financial information. This data will remain under seal, unless New York prosecutes and tries Trump for financial crimes.

After Trump's election as president, the General Services Administration (GSA) approved the then president-elect's continuing hold on a lease to the Old Post Office property in Washington, D.C., the site of Trump's International Hotel. He maintained his privilege to own, operate, and profit from the hotel. Yet to avoid conflict with the Constitution's Emoluments Clauses, the terms of the lease state, "No member or delegate to Congress, *or elected official of the Government of the United States* or the Government of the District of Columbia, shall be admitted to any share or part of this Lease, or to any benefit that may arise therefrom." Designed to avoid conflicts of interest between the GSA, which administers the lease, and other government officials, the provision is not gratuitous. The rental arrangement effectively made the president the concurrent tenant and landlord of the property.

"It's hard to imagine a more stark, compelling, or blatant conflict of interest," said Professor Stephen L. Schooner, an authority on government procurement at George Washington University. A January 2019 report by the Inspector General (IG) for the GSA concluded that the GSA "improperly ignored" the Emoluments Clause of the Constitution, "even though the lease itself requires compliance with the laws of the United States, including the Constitution. In addition, we found that GSA's unwillingness to address the constitutional issues affected its analysis . . . and the decision to grant Tenant" the lease.

Trump's arrangement with the GSA doubly violates the domestic Emoluments Clause. It gives the president a lease of great value and a source of payments for the hotel's services by the "United States or a State of the United States," according to the IG report. Secret Service agents lived at the hotel. Donald Trump Jr. stayed at the hotel while in Washington. His Secret Service detail reported paying $3,300 for rooms over two days.

Government spending at other Trump properties compounded violations of the domestic Emoluments Clause. Available records show that the federal government spent several million dollars at Trump properties. When Trump hosted Chinese President Xi Jinping at Mar-a-Lago in April 2017, he charged the U.S. government more than $7,000 for a thirty-person dinner. Trump charged the U.S. Secret Service $17,000 from May to November for rental of a cottage at his Bedminster, New Jersey, golf club, whether Trump or family members were present or not. The government paid to house Secret Service agents when Trump or family members traveled to his properties. This included trips by Eric Trump to the company's golf clubs in Scotland and Ireland, where he conducted paying tours of the properties. In breach of usual practice, Trump temporarily granted Secret Service protection for his four adult children and three former aides.

Business and political interests spent millions of dollars at Trump's properties, compounding conflicts of interest. Corporate interests included the Institute of International Bakers, groups representing the firearms industry, and the Community Financial Services Association, which represents major payday lenders. The National Mining Association, and T-Mobile, which was seeking regulatory approval to merge with Sprint, also patronized Trump properties.

More than 140 individual members of Congress accumulated over 360 visits to Trump properties during his presidency, according to an analysis by Citizens for Responsibility and Ethics in Washington (CREW). Some two hundred political groups have spent money at Trump properties. The patrons included Trump's own campaign committee and the Republican National Committee. Political action committees such as America First Action, Inc. and the Great America Committee patronized the venues. So did the campaign committees of Republicans such as House Minority Leader Kevin McCarthy; Indiana Representative Greg Pence, the older brother of Vice President Mike Pence; and Senator Tom Cotton. The 2020 Trump campaign likely poured far more money than disclosed into the pockets of Trump and family members. The campaign concealed $759 million of expenditures through routing to the dark money shell company, American Made Media Consultants, LLC.

Trump's receipt of the GSA lease for his D.C. hotel led to violations of the foreign Emoluments Clause, which the inspector general said "becomes relevant if the hotel receives payments from or on behalf of foreign governments, or a foreign instrumentality, when its representatives stay or hold events at the hotel or otherwise use its services." The pricey hotel became a magnet for foreign interests, who rent rooms and hold events on its grounds. The Philippine Embassy held its Independence Day celebration at the hotel in 2018, which was "a statement that we have a good relationship with this president," noted the Philippine ambassador.

The government of Cyprus held a three-day "Justice for Cyprus Conference" in May 2018 at Trump's hotel. The government-linked *Cyprus News Agency* said that Cyprus officials were seeking "ways of exerting influence on US President Donald Trump with a view to avert the Islamization of the Turkish-occupied part of Cyprus." Kuwait booked the Trump hotel for its National Day celebrations from 2017 to 2019. Three Trump cabinet members attended in 2019, along with White House senior advisor Kellyanne Conway. Azerbaijan, Bahrain, Ecuador, India, Malaysia, Saudi Arabia, and Turkey have all booked events or stays at the D.C. hotel.

An analysis by CREW found that for all Trump's properties, a minimum of 150 foreign officials from seventy-seven foreign governments had visited at least once. Twenty Trump officials attended a foreign government's event at a Trump property during his presidency. Trump had sought to hold the 2020 G-7 summit meeting at the Trump National Doral property in Miami until a public backlash forced him to back down. Trump had Vice President Mike Pence stay at his family's golf resort in Doonbeg, Ireland, during a 2019 visit. The vice president's official business was on the other side of the country.

As the Emoluments Clauses are not subject to penalties other than impeachment, CREW filed a civil suit against President Trump for violating the foreign Emoluments Clause. It petitioned the court for an injunction against the president to stop the violations. After a lower federal court dismissed the suit, the U.S. Court of Appeals for the Second Circuit reversed the ruling and remanded the case for further proceedings. Trump managed to prolong the litigation through the end of his presidency, after which the Supreme Court vacated as moot all lower court rulings.

The problem is that there was no clear line between Trump's private interests and the national interest. Did he defer to Russian president Vladimir Putin and Turkish president Recep Tayyip Erdogan due to financial interests in their countries? Did he absolve Crown Prince Mohammed bin Salman of the murder of American resident Jamal Khashoggi because of business dealings in Saudi Arabia? Did he accord special treatment to foreign and corporate interests that patronized his properties? Did his decisions on matters such as taxes, regulations, and employer-union relations impact his own bottom line? Fortunately, beyond endless litigation, there are statutory remedies to check conflicts of interest by presidents.

## THE FIX: A NEW CONFLICT OF INTEREST ACT

In a 1974 memo, future Supreme Court Justice Antonin Scalia, then a Justice Department attorney, said that presidents should voluntarily follow the conflict of interest rules that bind other federal officials. "It would obviously be undesirable as a matter of policy for the President or Vice President to engage in conduct proscribed by the Order or regulations," he wrote. "Failure to observe these standards will furnish a simple basis for damaging criticism, whether or not they technically apply."

The experience of the Trump presidency proves that voluntary compliance does not suffice. The nation needs a new conflict of interest law that covers the president and candidates for the presidency. The law would require that all declared presidential candidates disclose ten years of their latest tax returns. Disclosure would include all businesses under their control or in which they have substantial investments. The ongoing disclosure of tax returns would continue through a presidential administration and apply to a vice president who assumes the presidency.

The legislation would require presidents to report any transactions with foreign governments or their entities and agents during their term. It would require them to divest all their financial interests and place the resulting assets in a truly blind trust, managed by independent trustees. It would require political appointees to recuse themselves on matters that might affect the financial interests of the president. The act should codify into law the provisions of the foreign and domestic Emoluments Clauses and authorize civil suits for their enforcement. It should establish a new anti-corruption body with subpoena powers to investigate any conflicts of interest within the executive branch.

Congress should fortify the U.S. Office of Government Ethics (OGE), which oversees conflicts of interest and other ethical transgressions. Lawmakers should order the dismissal of the office's director only for cause. They should follow the pattern of other regulatory bodies and allocate funds that do not need to be reviewed by the president's Office of Management and Budget. They should empower the OGE with civil enforcement power like that of other regulators. The OGE should have the authority to conduct investigations with subpoena power and to seek civil penalties against federal officials in federal court. While penalties would not apply to the president, restrictions on members of the White House staff and other senior officials would restrain ethics violations by the chief executive.

# • 8 •

# Political Cleansing

*Stopping Favoritism, Cronyism, and Nepotism*

I'm going to surround myself only with the best and most serious people. We want top of the line professionals.

—Presidential candidate Donald J. Trump, 2015

*In* 1920, Republican Senator Warren Harding of Ohio, an improbable candidate, best known for womanizing and poker playing, won the presidency in the greatest landslide by a challenging candidate in U.S. history. Harding made some outstanding appointments such as Charles Evans Hughes as Secretary of State and Herbert Hoover as Secretary of Commerce. But his tenure, which fell into scandal and disgrace, illustrates the dangers of appointing cronies, friends, and political allies.

Harding named his friend, Republican Senator Albert Fall of New Mexico, as Interior Secretary. He disregarded conservationists who opposed Fall's philosophy of uncontrolled capitalism. Harding appointed his campaign manager and confidant, Harry Daugherty, as Attorney General. He dismissed the concerns of Republican Senators about Daugherty's character. "I have told [Daugherty] that he can have any place in my Cabinet he wants, outside of Secretary of State," Harding said. "He tells me that he wants to be Attorney General, and by God, he will be Attorney General!" Harding made his friend and political ally Charles Forbes head of the Veterans Bureau. He put in Albert D. Lasker, a donor and 1920 campaign official as Chair of the United States Shipping Board, and another crony, Thomas W. Miller, as Alien Property Custodian. His office controlled "all money and property in the United States due or belonging to an enemy, or ally of an enemy."

Private oilmen bribed Fall for access to petroleum held in government reserves at Elk Hills, California, and Teapot Dome, Wyoming. Fall became the first American cabinet member to serve a prison term for official corruption, and commentators dubbed the Harding scandals "Teapot Dome." Federal prosecutors charged Daugherty with bribery in the sale of assets confiscated during the First World War. He twice escaped conviction through hung juries. Only one juror held out for acquittal in the second trial. A public outcry eventually forced President Harding to dismiss Daugherty. Forbes served a year and eight months in prison for conspiracy to defraud the U.S. Government. Congressional critics accused Lasker of "throwing our ships away" by selling surplus vessels at the bargain-basement price of $30 per ton, but prosecutors did not charge him with a crime. Miller spent eighteen months in prison for plotting to defraud the government.

A U.S. Supreme Court decision following these scandals authorized Congress to investigate violations of the law by subpoena. In 1924, Congress authorized certain congressional committees with jurisdiction over federal taxes to acquire information on federal tax returns. This is the law that gave rise to extended litigation when President Trump's appointees resisted a subpoena from the House Ways and Means committee for his tax returns.

Trump, like Harding, appointed government officials based on their personal loyalty and political ties, not on their competence or honesty. Unlike Harding, though, Trump dealt vindictively with allegedly disloyal appointees, including National Security Council staff member Alexander Vindman and Ukrainian ambassador Marie Yovanovitch. After voting to acquit President Trump in his first Senate trial, Republican Susan Collins of Maine said, "I believe that the President has learned from this case" and "will be much more cautious in the future." She was wrong. Trump looked upon his acquittal as a license to extend his political purge of government. Donald Trump Jr. admitted that the impeachment process helped in "unearthing who all needed to be fired."

Alexander Vindman lived the American dream until he clashed with Donald Trump. His widowed father fled to the United States from the Ukrainian Republic of the Soviet Union in 1979 with his three-year-old twin boys, Alexander and Yevgeny, and their older brother, Leonid. Alexander earned a master's degree from Harvard University in Russian, Eastern European, and Central Asian studies.

He became a U.S. citizen, and joined the military as a commissioned officer. The military awarded him a purple heart for combat injuries in Iraq and four other commendations.

Vindman rose to the rank of Lieutenant Colonel in 2015 and in 2018 assumed his dream position as an Eastern European expert on the National Security Council. During Trump's first impeachment, Vindman did "his duty." He testified truthfully about what he had personally observed about President Trump's efforts to entice Ukrainian President Volodymyr Zelensky to announce politically beneficial inquiries. Vindman testified, "In Russia, my act of . . . offering public testimony involving the president would surely cost me my life." In America, he said, "I will be fine for telling the truth."

Vindman was not fine. President Trump fired him from the National Security Council and simultaneously pushed his brother out of another White House position. It did not end there. The White House interfered with Vindman's scheduled promotion to full colonel. With no future in the military, Vindman resigned his commission. It was not enough for Trump to derail Vindman's career. He had to punish disloyalty by sullying Vindman with lies and insinuations. The president tweeted, "he was very insubordinate, reported contents of my 'perfect' calls incorrectly, &. was given a horrendous report by his superior, the man he reported to, who publicly stated that Vindman had problems with judgement, adhering to the chain of command and leaking information. In other words, 'OUT'." Former Republican Representative Sean Duffy suggested that Vindman was more loyal to Ukraine than the United States. Fox News commentator Laura Ingraham insinuated that "we have a U.S. national security official who is advising Ukraine while working inside the White House, apparently against the president's interests."

"I made the difficult decision to retire," Vindman said, "because a campaign of bullying, intimidation and retaliation by President Trump and his allies forever limited the progression of my military career." He said that he joined "dozens of other lifelong public servants who have left this administration with their integrity intact but their careers irreparably harmed." Vindman was right. "Our national government during the past few years," Vindman said, "has been more reminiscent of the authoritarian regime my family fled more than forty years ago than the country I have devoted my life to serving."

Trump targeted for dismissal and retaliation Marie Yovanovitch, the respected career ambassador to Ukraine, who began serving her country under President Ronald Reagan. Trump worried that Yovanovitch, a renowned anti-corruption crusader, would impede his pressure campaign in Ukraine. Trump's personal attorney Rudy Giuliani, who had conducted a rogue foreign policy operation in Ukraine, orchestrated a smear campaign against Yovanovitch. Giuliani fabricated stories that she was blocking the prosecution of corruption in Ukraine and working politically against the Trump administration.

Trump fired Yovanovitch in April 2019, and in his call to Ukrainian President Zelensky disparaged her as "bad news." During her testimony in the House impeachment inquiry, Trump tweeted, "Everywhere Marie Yovanovitch went turned bad." To his undying shame, Secretary of State Mike Pompeo stayed blindly loyal to President Trump and said not a word to defend his employee from the hatchet job on her character and service. Without a future in the Trump administration, Yovanovitch quit the foreign service in January 2020.

The firing and disparagement of Vindman and Yovanovitch fit within an approach to governing that put personal loyalty to Trump above fidelity to the law, the Constitution, and the good of the country. George Washington fretted about government through favoritism or cronyism. A president must "discharge the duties of the office with that impartiality and zeal for the public good," he wrote, "which ought never to suffer connections of blood or friendship to intermingle." Instead, merit must guide appointment. "My political conduct in nominations . . . must be exceedingly circumspect and proof against just criticism," he said. Decades later Speaker of the U.S. House Henry Clay said, "government is a trust, and the officers of the government are trustees; and both the trust and the trustees are created for the benefit of the people."

Contrary to these admonitions, patronage appointments and kickbacks became routine practice in the nineteenth century, until Congress reformed the federal service in 1883. The federal government was a skeletal operation in those days. Most federal employees ran post offices; presidents controlled few political appointees and lacked a White House staff. Presidents relied on a few secretaries and administrative assistants. The federal government grew exponentially in the twentieth century. Today, it employs approximately 2.1 million non-military personnel. The White House staff numbers some four hundred persons, and presidents get to make several thousand political appointments. Before Trump, George W. Bush used his appointment power to subjugate the public service to his will. Bush inserted political loyalists in government posts to circumvent the work of professional career civil servants. At the Food and Drug Administration, for example, Bush's political appointees excluded career staff from making decisions or even providing meaningful input. "There was a steady erosion of influence by the career staff beginning in January of '01, and by maybe late '02 the careers were largely excluded and powerless in decision making," said William Hubbard, who retired as associate commissioner for policy and planning in spring 2005 after more than twenty-five years at the FDA. Bush's political loyalists "operate with a single-minded focus that makes them very present in the day-to-day operation of the agencies, all the way down to the field levels," said Paul Light, professor of Public Service at New York University.

Bush created new positions for his operatives within the government. A report by Democratic Representative Henry Waxman revealed that during his first five years, Bush added 307 new political appointees to the federal payroll. He increased Schedule C political appointments, which do not require Senate approval, by 33 percent. "The number of layers being created at the top of the federal government has increased dramatically under Bush," said Professor Light. Under Bush, "politics is injected and elevated in decisions where science and rational judgment should prevail," said Rick Melberth, director of regulatory policy at the nonpartisan Office of Management and Budget (OMB) Watch. "Politics supersedes scientific and technical information."

Bush politicized the merit-based public service by making politically based hiring decisions. "Many of the politicization scandals in this administration came from cases where unqualified or inexperienced people got into key jobs . . . often with the power to hire others or control information flows," said political science professor David E. Lewis of Vanderbilt University. A study published in the *Review of Public Personnel Administration* found that in the departments of Defense and Homeland Security, Bush had expanded political control over hiring and firing and weakened union protections for civil servants. "It seems clear that ideological and political motives were at play and dominated technical concerns," the researchers concluded. "Bush's political aims as an orthodox innovator were nothing less than a political realignment toward Republicanism in the United States that would last for a generation and complete the Reagan Revolution," they said. However, blowback from unions, the courts, the Democratic majority that took over Congress in 2007, and the new administration of President Barack Obama in 2009 blunted the long-term effects of Bush's personnel changes.

No president before Trump, including George W. Bush, has so brazenly bent public service to his political will. His abuses exposed still-gaping holes in the latitude for presidential hiring and firing in the modern era of big government. It starts with nepotism under Trump. Not since John F. Kennedy appointed his brother Robert F. Kennedy as attorney general and his brother-in-law Sargent Shriver as director of the Peace Corps has any president brought immediate family members into their administration. Trump named his daughter Ivanka Trump and her husband, Jared Kushner, to top White House posts, despite their lack of qualifications. Trump's advisors said the 1967 anti-nepotism statute, adopted in the wake of Kennedy's designations, did not cover the White House. Besides, the wealthy couple waived their government salary. Ivanka and Jared made up to $640 million while in government service.

Trump's nepotism did not stop there. He appointed Andrew Giuliani, the son of his personal lawyer Rudy Giuliani, as a special assistant to the president. He named Tyler McGaughey, the son-in-law of Attorney General William Barr, as an associate in the White House counsel's office, and Mary Daly, Barr's daughter, as a senior advisor to the director of the Treasury Department's financial crimes unit. Eric Trump's brother-in-law, Kyle Yunaska, served as Deputy Chief of Staff at NASA Headquarters.

Trump extended his purges of offending officials to top-level FBI officials who had investigated him and his campaign: Deputy Director Andrew McCabe, Chief Counsel James Baker, and FBI Director James Comey. Like Vindman and Yovanovitch, Trump set out to destroy them personally, a transparent warning to any government official who would not do his bidding. No prior president had ever stooped so low. He fired McCabe just twenty-six hours before he would retire and vest in his government pension. Trump tweeted about McCabe, who was scarcely a household name, more than forty times. He accused McCabe of engaging in a "treasonous" plot against the president. Trump's Justice Department referred for criminal prosecution allegations that McCabe had lied about a media contact. For about two years, the case remained suspended like a sword of Damocles over McCabe's head. Justice finally ended it without charge or explanation.

Trump publicly disparaged Comey more than a hundred times. He said, "Comey will now officially go down as the worst leader, by far, in the history of the FBI. I did a great service to the people in firing him." He called Comey "slippery," a "slimeball," and a "dirty cop" who "got caught." A report by Justice's inspector general found that the FBI's investigations of the Trump campaign did not suffer from "political bias or improper motivation."

Trump fired or forced the resignation of his other suspect appointees. He led a revolving-door government, which set a turnover record. Trump dismissed or accepted the resignation of some four hundred high-level political appointees. He had fourteen turnovers in his cabinet, compared to three for Barack Obama and two for George W. Bush in their first terms. Within the White House, the departed included three chiefs of staff, six communications directors, and four national security advisors.

Trump's former campaign manager and White House chief strategist Steve Bannon had convinced the president that the federal workers were part of a "deep state" which would destroy Trump unless he destroyed it first. Bannon had perverted the concept of the "deep state," which actually referred to a cabal of lobbyists, defense contractors, multinational corporations, and banks who exploited government for their own selfish ends. Trump himself, who boasted about controlling politicians with his campaign contributions, exemplified the deep state. "When you give, they do whatever the hell you want them to do," he said in 2015.

"Ours is a government of checks and balances," the late comedian Steve Allen quipped. "The Mafia and crooked businessmen make out checks, and the politicians and other compromised officials improve their bank balances." A shattering study by political scientists Martin Gilens and Benjamin Page found that wealthy individuals like Donald Trump and business-dominated interest groups control the policies of government. As compared to the power of economic elites, the influence of ordinary Americans, registered at a "non-significant, near-zero level." These elites and their allies in government constitute the real deep state that President Trump has abetted with his tax cuts, his dismantling of pro-consumer and environmental regulations, and his assembling of the wealthiest cabinet in history. To conceal this bias, Bannon and Trump conjured up the myth of a so-called swamp that he pledged to drain away.

As a complement to his purges, Trump relied on acting appointments, without Senate confirmation, to stock the government with officials loyal only to him. Trump made more interim appointments than any other president. The *Washington Post* reported in early 2020 that, "'acting' officials in the Trump administration have held down 22 Cabinet and Cabinet-level jobs for a combined 2,700 days—about 1 out of every 9 days across those jobs." This accounted for more than seven years of acting service, about triple the number for President Obama's first term. Alexander Hamilton had stressed the importance of Senate confirmation in the Constitution as "an excellent check upon a spirit of favoritism in the President," that "would tend greatly to prevent the appointment of unfit characters from State prejudice, from family connection, from personal attachment, or from a view to popularity."

In August 2020, the Government Accountability Office (GAO) found that President Trump had broken the law in appointing Chad Wolf as acting secretary of the Department of Homeland Security (DHS) and Ken Cuccinelli as acting "Senior Official Performing the Duties of Deputy Secretary." The DHS had lacked a Senate-confirmed secretary since Kirstjen Nielsen, who resigned in April 2019. Of twenty-seven senior positions at DHS, ten were filled by acting officials. Among key positions across the federal service, as of mid-August 2020, 65 percent remained unfilled at Homeland Security, 55 percent at Justice, 43 percent at EPA, 36 percent at Defense, and 24 percent at State.

In September 2020, another federal judge ordered the removal of William Perry Pendley, who had been serving as acting director of the Bureau of Land Management for over a year. "The President cannot shelter unconstitutional 'temporary' appointments for the duration of his presidency through a *matryoshka* [Russian nesting doll] of delegated authorities," U.S. District Judge Brian Morris ruled.

By outsourcing government functions to private, for-profit companies Trump further weakened the federal workforce and diminished accountability. A June 2019 analysis by the independent National Employment Law Project found that in 2018, the Trump administration spent $1.7 billion on private temporary help contracts, more than double the $812 million from the Obama administration's last year. "The Trump administration and its allies in Congress are merely outsourcing government work to temporary staffing agencies, which degrades the quality of those jobs and reduces accountability over the quality of that work," the report concluded.

The Trump administration also outsourced more lasting projects, such as detention facilities for Immigration and Customs Enforcement prisoners. Investigations uncovered widespread abuse and neglect at these private facilities. During the pandemic, the administration outsourced to private companies the provision of personal protective equipment and coronavirus tests. This resulted in shortages and forced states to compete in private markets, increasing the cost of supplies.

Following Bush's example, Trump politicized the traditionally non-partisan and professional public service. Every employee under Trump, from lawyers at Justice, to accountants at Treasury, and scientists at the EPA, owed personal loyalty to their boss. Employees found that their expertise was often unused or exploited. Unlike the meat packing plants in Upton Sinclair's novel *The Jungle*, work in Trump's departments and agencies was not life-threatening. But civil servants still described it as grim and burdensome. Trump presided over a weakened and demoralized civil service with reduced effectiveness, as revealed in interviews with career employees.

Erica Newland, an attorney in the Office of Legal Counsel, said that "there was hardly any respect for the other departments of government—not for the lower courts, not for Congress, and certainly not for the bureaucracy, for professionalism, for facts or the truth." Yet, "there was no sense that there was anything to be gained by standing up within the office." One of her supervisors said, "We're just following orders." He added, "I know that's what the Nazis said, but we're not Nazis."

In anonymous interviews, career civil servants still in the bureaucracy made similar complaints. An employee at Treasury said, "Generally, [previous] secretaries have respected career staff. I think we took pride in being above politics. Here, that was completely disregarded to make a political point. . . . I want to leave because I think what I'm do-ing—while not terrible—is not particularly constructive, and I could be more useful outside the government."

A professional at the Office of Management and Budget said, "There's not enough for us to do, and Trump's appointees don't want us involved in the decision-making anyway. . . . I really care about trying to make things better, and it sucks feeling like I can't do that anymore." A civil servant at State said, "This administration feels like a free-for-all, and whatever process we do have almost feels like a waste of time, since we know Trump will just decide to do whatever he feels like. Morale is pretty low, and I think it has to do with the general lack of respect for civil servants."

An employee of the National Labor Relations Board said, "A lot of the regions are now badly understaffed. The appointees offered early retirement to clericals who had been here for, like, forty years. Those people had massive institutional knowledge. . . . Now the administra-tion is trying to backfill with people they can pay a lot less and who have a lot less experience. It's like they said, 'Let's buy out the people who could effectively thwart us.'" A scientist at the EPA said, "there's a contingent of Republicans who view environmental protection as some kind of leftist conspiracy to make American corporations less competi-tive. . . . Our budget has been declining almost as long as I've been here, but under Trump, it went into overdrive."

Trump dismissed independent inspectors general who investigate waste, incompetence, and corruption in federal agencies. He dismissed Inspector General (IG) Michael Atkinson, who took the whistle-blower's complaint on Trump's Ukrainian coercion to Congress. Trump claimed without evidence that Atkinson "did a terrible job." He said that "he took a fake report and brought it to Congress with an emergency. Okay? Not a big Trump fan, I can tell you." Atkinson "never came in to see me" before forwarding the whistleblower complaint, Trump said.

Yet, the complaint accurately tracked Trump's call with Zelensky and his withholding of military aid to Ukraine. The whistleblower law required Atkinson to bring the complaint to Congress, not the presi-dent, who was the subject of its allegations. "It is hard not to think that the president's loss of confidence in me derives from my having faith-fully discharged my legal obligations as an independent and impartial inspector general," Atkinson said. Trump maligned the anonymous whistleblower as a "traitor" who should suffer the "old days" remedy of execution.

Trump fired the Inspector General for Transportation, Michael Behm; for Defense, Glenn Fine; for Health and Human Services, Christi Grimm; and for State, Steve Linick. Trump did not justify these firings for good cause, but claimed, "I think we've been treated very unfairly by inspectors general." Translation: They did not just bow to his will, like so many obedient Stepford wives. Trump falsely claimed that "I think every president has gotten rid of probably more than I have." In the sixteen years of their two terms combined, Presidents Obama and Bush fired only one inspector general. Benjamin Wittes of Lawfare wrote that Trump's IG firings typified his use of presidential "power to vindictively fire investigators and staffers who don't 'protect' him."

In addition to firing independent-minded IGs, the president impeded investigations of his administration. A refusal to release documents and communications by Trump appointees delayed for years investigations of the administration's response to Hurricane Maria's devastation of Puerto Rico; its potential exposure of federal employees to COVID-19; its contracts for building Trump's border wall; its failure to control cancer-causing emissions; and its efforts to place a citizenship question in the Census.

Similar obstruction delayed other reports until after the election. Investigators found that White House physician Ronny Jackson had bullied his staff and drank on the job and that former Transportation Secretary Elaine Chao and former Secretary of State Mike Pompeo misused their positions by using paid staff for personal business. After a three-year delay, a report on Commerce Secretary Wilbur Ross's finances found that he had misled federal officials about his assets and stock distributions. It did not conclude that Ross had lied intentionally. Trump political appointees at Justice long delayed and eventually stymied investigations of alleged ethics violations by former Interior Secretary Ryan Zinke. A Trump loyalist and political appointee blocked investigations of how COVID-19 had spread within the Secret Service and the Service's response to peaceful demonstrations in Washington, D.C.

In June 2020, a Trump appointee, the conservative documentary filmmaker Michael Pack, became head of the U.S. Agency for Global Media. The agency supervises international broadcast media such as the flagship Voice of America. Pack assumed the mission of turning his agency into a pro-Trump propaganda machine. He fired most of the leadership, installed Trump loyalists, and disbanded a bipartisan oversight board. Pack insisted that editorials and reporting conform to Trump's priorities. He rescinded rules that protected journalists under his watch from political interference. Through a no-bid contract, Pack paid a law firm more than two million taxpayer dollars to investigate and discredit his senior executives.

Five fired career employees at Voice of America sued in federal court for an injunction to block Pack's political tampering. In November 2020, Federal District Court Judge Beryl Howell enjoined Pack from "making or interfering with personnel decisions for journalists," from "communicating with editors and journalists . . . regarding journalistic or editorial matters without the consent of the head of their network." The order barred him from investigating "journalistic content, individual editors or journalists, or alleged editorial lapses or breaches of journalistic ethics." On December 2, 2020, the U.S. Office of Special Counsel disclosed "a substantial likelihood of wrongdoing" on Pack's watch. It charged "gross mismanagement" by Pack and breaches of the legal firewall that protects journalistic integrity.

During the 2020 campaign, many administration appointees used their official positions to promote Trump's candidacy. This activity violated the Hatch Act, which prohibits administration officials other than the president or vice president from using their government positions or assets in partisan campaigns. Ivanka Trump repeatedly used her official Twitter account on behalf of her father's campaign. For instance, she tweeted, "Barnstorming the Fox cities today! The great people of Wisconsin delivered for @RealDonaldTrump in 2016 and will do it again!" She added, "Mail-in voting has already begun—to get everything you need to cast your vote for President Trump visit votedonaldjtrump. com." Jared Kushner, the *New York Times* reported, became "the person officially overseeing the entire [Trump] campaign from his office in the West Wing, organizing campaign meetings and making decisions about staffing and spending."

On his official Twitter account and during interviews in his capacity as Director of Trade and Manufacturing Policy, Peter Navarro relentlessly attacked Trump's opponents, Joe Biden and Kamala Harris. He charged Biden with being "compromised" and "bought" by China and called him "Beijing Biden." He smeared Harris as "just a mouth-piece" and said, "I can't really take her seriously." Other administration officials campaigned for Trump in their official capacity. Agriculture Secretary Sonny Purdue, on a government-paid official trip to North Carolina, pleaded for Trump's reelection. "We've never seen an out-pouring of compassion like that for people who matter, because people matter to you," Perdue said. "And that's what's important to me. And that's what's gonna continue to happen—four more years—if America gets out and votes for this man, Donald J. Trump."

Senior executives breached the Hatch Act at the Republican National Nominating Convention, which for the first time a president held at the White House. The convention featured a video of acting Homeland Security Secretary Chad Wolf, in his official capacity, swearing in new U.S. citizens at the White House, while Trump looked on with approval. Mike Pompeo became the first sitting Secretary of State to deliver a convention speech. He did so during an official state visit to Israel.

White House Chief of Staff Mark Meadows dismissed findings of Hatch Act violations. "Nobody outside of the Beltway really cares," he said. The American people should be concerned if federal officials are abusing their taxpayer-funded jobs for partisan ends. However, an impotent Office of Special Counsel, which enforces the Hatch Act, did not impose a single penalty on an offender. It issued warnings or referred violators to the White House, which amounts to putting a fox in charge of henhouse security.

As Trump's term expired, the lame duck president removed apostate appointees, while bringing new acolytes to the government. He fired Director of the Cybersecurity and Infrastructure Security Agency Christopher Krebs, Defense Secretary Mark Esper, and the Defense Undersecretary for Intelligence Joseph Kernan. He accepted a resignation from Attorney General William Barr. Trump made more than one hundred lame duck appointments and nominations, with little attention to experience or expertise. He installed his former campaign manager Corey Lewandowski and his deputy David Bossie on the Pentagon's Defense Business Board after removing such luminaries as former Secretaries of State Henry Kissinger and Madeleine Albright. He appointed Acting Undersecretary of Defense for Policy Anthony Tata to an advisory board position at the Merchant Marine Academy. Tata had a history of inflammatory remarks that precluded his confirmation by the Senate.

To avoid the efficient cancellation of appointments by incoming President Biden, Trump buried dozens of political appointees in civil service positions. "To the extent that a president tries to use his own authority to pressure executive branch officials to be loyal to him rather than to the law, that undermines on a fundamental level the governmental structure that we've set up," said University of Washington law professor Lisa Manheim. Miles Taylor, the former chief of staff for Trump's Department of Homeland Security, described from the inside how Trump's political manipulations had subverted the department's mission. He said, "What we saw week in and week out, and for me, after two and a half years in that administration, was terrifying. We would go in to try to talk to him about a pressing national security issue—cyberattack, terrorism threat—he wasn't interested in those things. To him, they weren't priorities." Instead, "The president has tried to turn DHS, the nation's largest law enforcement agency, into a tool used for his political benefit."

### THE FIX: RESTRICT ACTING APPOINTMENTS, ENFORCE THE HATCH ACT, APPLY ANTI-NEPOTISM LAWS TO THE WHITE HOUSE, CUT POLITICAL APPOINTMENTS, PROTECT INSPECTORS GENERAL, TIGHTEN WHISTLEBLOWER LAWS, AND STRENGTHEN DISCLOSURE

To curb the abuses of acting appointments, Congress should limit acting officials to a maximum tenure of 120 days from the date of the vacancy and disallow multiple periods of service. It should compel interim appointees to appear before Congress at least once every sixty days, alternating between the House and Senate oversight committees. Congress should strengthen the offices of inspectors general by increasing funding and requiring relevant experience and qualifications. It should specify firing offenses and make sure that a president documents his reasons for dismissals. New law should apply anti-nepotism restrictions to White House personnel and prohibit government employees from signing non-disclosure agreements.

Additional reforms should reduce the number of political appointees from the current unmanageable four thousand. Studies have shown that political appointees often lack the skills, competence, and institutional knowledge of career public servants. They are less inclined to put the public good above politics. The proliferation of political appointments contributes to the revolving door of government employment through at-will, presidential firing. A new act should make a clear distinction between public service positions and federal appointees so that a president cannot bury loyalists in the protected bureaucracy.

Congress should reduce the outsourcing of government functions to private organizations, such as for-profit prison businesses. All government service contracts should be discontinued within six months. Renewal should depend on a performance and cost-benefit review by the Office of Management and Budget, with oversight by the House and Senate budget committees. Reform legislation should strengthen prohibitions against the awarding of no-bid contracts and specify a code of conduct for government contractors. It should enact educational and skill requirements or mandatory training for new hires and rewrite the outmoded civil service code to make it easier to recruit and retain highly skilled workers.

Congress should provide permanent access for whistleblowers to bypass the currently ineffective Merit Systems Protection Board (MSPB) and apply directly for relief in any federal court from retaliatory action. As of early 2020, the MSPB had a backlog of more than two thousand cases. Congress should establish an independent auditor to hear complaints about reprisals, with referral power to the courts. It should give members of the intelligence community and the military the same protections as whistleblowers in other agencies.

Congress needs to put muscle and teeth into the Hatch Act. It should increase funding and staffing for the neglected Office of Special Counsel. It should empower the office to investigate any suspected Hatch Act violation regardless of complaints and clarify that the act applies to all White House officials.

# · 9 ·

# Governing in the Dark

## *Expanding Transparency*

Without publicity, no good is permanent; under the auspices of publicity, no evil can continue.

—English philosopher Jeremy Bentham, 1768

$\mathscr{A}$fter his landslide victory in the presidential election of 1964, President Lyndon Johnson secretly deliberated with his advisors about sending U.S. combat troops to Vietnam. The president decided to intervene in Vietnam without the expectation of winning a war there. Rather, he hoped to achieve a negotiated settlement by raising the costs of war for the North Vietnamese. Johnson told his cabinet, "Our objective is just that: It is to convince them that they can't win there. We think we can achieve this objective by moving toward a stalemate, convincing them that the situation in the South will not lead to a military victory." Johnson led his nation to war with a goal that dared not speak its name in public: stalemate. He could not ask Americans to risk their lives to tie one for the Gipper. Had Johnson been transparent about his objective, he would likely have failed to muster public support for a war that America ultimately lost at a cost of nearly sixty thousand American lives and likely more than a million Asian lives.

In *The Twilight of the Presidency*, George Reedy, Lyndon Johnson's former press secretary, pointed to the fallacy behind this lack of transparency: "the insidious belief that the president and a few of his most trusted advisers are possessed of a special knowledge that must be closely held within a small group." Closed-door decision making on a matter of great public import, he explained, led to disastrous decisions on the Vietnam War. Decisions might have come out differently if leaders were "put to the test of defending [their] positions in public debate." A lack of transparency, Reedy explained, works in opposition to the national interest.

America's Framers recognized the need for executive branch secrecy in circumstances such as negotiating treaties or formulating battlefield plans. But they insisted that while secrecy should sometimes be deep, such exceptions are limited, and that generally secrecy should be shallow. Hamilton backed a unitary executive in part because his decisions would be most open to public inspection, including "opportunity of discovering [misconduct] with facility and clearness." One person "will be more narrowly watched and most readily suspected." Thomas Jefferson wrote that "whenever the people are well-informed, they can be trusted with their government, for whenever things go so far wrong as to attract their notice, they can be relied on to set things right." James Madison said that "a popular Government without popular information, or the means of acquiring it, is but a Prologue to a Farce or a Tragedy, or perhaps both. Knowledge will forever govern ignorance: And a people who mean to be their own Governors, must arm themselves with the power which knowledge gives."

Before Johnson, two earlier presidents, Woodrow Wilson and Harry Truman, initiated the excessive modern practice of executive secrecy. During the First World War, President Wilson issued covert orders for cabinet heads to fire government employees whose retention was "injurious to the public interest." He secretly authorized the War Department to monitor international communications. Wilson kept virtually all military information secret, disregarding the public's right to know about his conduct of the war. After the war, his attorney general covertly investigated suspected radicals and agitators.

President Truman backed the National Security Act of 1947 that established the Central Intelligence Agency. It had the authority not only to gather and analyze intelligence, but also to conduct covert operations around the world. The act established the National Security Council, whose members are accountable only to the president, without confirmation by the Senate. A large part of the United States' international policies and practices became invisible to the public. Truman authorized secret monitoring of the "loyalty" of federal employees and covertly investigated alleged radicals. By executive order, Truman created the National Security Agency as another invisible body to conduct communications intelligence abroad. As revealed decades later, the NSA and the CIA had secretly monitored alleged dissidents in the United States.

President Truman initiated the modern system of document classification in 1951 by extending Wilson's order on military information to "all departments and agencies of the Executive Branch of the Government," with considerable discretion for the executive. Although future presidential decrees restricted the scope of covered agencies and provided for declassification, the process suffers from endemic overclassification. Administrations have kept many millions of government documents from public scrutiny for political, not security reasons. Thomas Blanton, director of the National Security Archive at George Washington University, testified before Congress in 2016 that "50 to 90 percent of the time" classifications "are wrong."

Despite his secret deliberations on going to war in Vietnam, President Johnson expanded transparency when he signed the Freedom of Information Act in 1966. It authorized any person to request executive branch records. The act had nine exceptions, including certain national security documents, privileged trade secrets or financial data, certain medical or law enforcement information, and any information excluded by statute.

President Ronald Reagan's CIA Director William J. Casey, through "Project Democracy," launched a flagrant attempt at governing in the dark. Through this sustainable, self-funded "government within the government," Casey and his associates would influence American public opinion, manipulate government officials, and conduct missions in secret. The point man for the Project, Lieutenant Colonel Oliver North of the National Security Council, said that the conspirators had built an "off-the-shelf, self-sustaining, stand-alone entity that could perform certain activities on behalf of the United States"—the ultimate version of an invisible "deep state."

No federal authority controlled the secret project, not the president nor Congress, not the Departments of Defense, State, or Justice. The conspirators had most notoriously sold arms to Iran and illegally diverted the profits to the Contra movement that that was battling a left-wing government in Nicaragua. Independent Counsel Lawrence Walsh, after seven years of investigation, could not pin down what Reagan knew about Project Democracy. Still, the president "created the conditions which made possible the crimes committed by others," who operated in "extreme secrecy" and "without accountability," Walsh concluded.

President George W. Bush struck further blows against transparency. In 2001, the first year of his presidency, Bush banned by decree the publication of records of previous administrations, unless authorized by the former president. The 9/11 attacks that year gave the administration cover for withholding information on the war it waged against terror and its justifications for authorizing torture and the warrantless wiretapping of American citizens. The administration erased information on transportation and energy from government websites and limited responses to Freedom of Information requests. It both expanded the classification of documents and restricted their declassification. From 2000 to 2007, classification actions increased from eleven million to over twenty-three million. Vice President Dick Cheney resisted a request from the General Accounting Office (now the Government Accountability Office) for basic information on meetings of his energy task force. After years of litigation, the courts upheld Cheney's prerogative to withhold the information.

The Obama administration fulfilled its pledge to increase transparency, but with caveats. It expanded the disclosure of national security information and responses to Freedom of Information requests. It limited the classification of government documents and reversed Bush's order on restricting access to presidential records. However, the administration punished whistleblowers and leakers who sought to expose government misconduct. It concealed information about many hundreds of drone strikes directed against alleged terrorists. Obama held far fewer individual or joint press conferences than his predecessors Bush and Clinton. His Department of Justice secretly seized phone records for reporters and editors at the Associated Press. Of thirty-five promises that Obama made to expand transparency, Politifact rated twelve as "Promise Broken."

Throughout American history, presidents have concealed their health challenges, starting with George Washington. In 1790, Washington began to suffer from a respiratory disease that probably threatened his life. "The physicians disclosed that they had no hopes of his recovery," wrote one eyewitness. The doctors treated Washington secretly. As explained by Abigail Adams, the wife of Vice President John

Adams, "It was thought prudent to say very little upon the Subject as a general alarm may have proved injurious to the present State of the government." Word of the president's illness still leaked to the press, but not his brush with death. Washington later reflected on his "several weeks of severe illness that nearly terminated my existence."

Physicians diagnosed President Chester A. Arthur in 1882 with Bright's disease, an often-fatal kidney disorder. When the *New York Herald* disclosed his affliction, the president's spokesperson issued a blanket denial. Arthur died four years later in November 1886. President Grover Cleveland's surgeons operated surreptitiously on his cancer of the jaw aboard a friend's yacht. However, reporter E. J. Edwards broke the true story of Cleveland's surgery on the *Philadelphia Press*'s front page under the headline, "The President A Very Sick Man." Cleveland rallied his allies and doctors to deny the story and discredit Edwards.

In 1919, President Woodrow Wilson went to the Palace of Versailles, near Paris, to negotiate a peace treaty with his European allies in the First World War. Wilson sought to persuade the European leaders to accept his idealistic Fourteen Points program of open diplomacy; freedom of the seas; unfettered trade; arms reduction; self-determination of peoples; an end to colonialism; and the establishment of a league of nations. In April, with negotiations stalled, Wilson contracted the Spanish flu. His temperature soared to 103 degrees, and he remained bedridden for five days. Wilson's personal physician, Dr. Cary Grayson, misled the press when he said that Wilson had contracted a cold, not the flu. Wilson returned to the negotiations weakened in body and mind, without the stamina or determination to impose his will on the conference. John Barry, the author of *The Great Influenza*, said, "The impact was pretty dramatic in my view. Wilson had been adamant, insisting on the '14 Points.'" Then, "all of a sudden, Wilson caved in on all 14 points except the League of Nations."

After returning home, Wilson suffered debilitating strokes while campaigning for the league. Wilson's physician kept even the vice president and the Congress in the dark about his affliction. It was a "great camouflage," in the words of White House Chief Usher Ike Hoover. Wilson remained impaired for nearly the last year and a half of his term. He could not deal effectively with the many postwar challenges confronting the country. Wilson's bizarre behavior prompted the

House Judiciary Committee to hold hearings on presidential disability, although not on his health per se. In a foreshadowing of the Twenty-Fifth Amendment, members proposed authorizing the cabinet or the Supreme Court to declare the president unfit for duty and authorizing the vice president to become acting president. The bills would apply only after Wilson completed his current term in 1921. Without consensus, though, Congress did not act.

When Franklin Roosevelt ran for a fourth term in 1944, physicians diagnosed him with life-threatening acute congestive heart failure. Dr. Frank Lahey, director of the Lahey Clinic in Boston, believed that FDR would not survive another presidency. Yet Roosevelt's personal physician, Admiral Ross T. McIntire, deceptively told reporters that FDR was in "excellent condition for a man of his age." With rumors of the president's affliction swirling in political circles, his Republican opponent, Tom Dewey, rejected a plea by some GOP strategists to make FDR's health an issue in the presidential campaign. Roosevelt died on April 12, 1945, soon after his fourth inauguration, at the age of sixty-three. A poorly informed and unprepared Vice President Harry Truman became president.

President John F. Kennedy struggled with severe back pain that kept him on painkillers. He suffered from Addison's disease, a chronic endocrine disorder that required regular doses of corticosteroids. Kennedy had stomach and colon ailments, urinary tract infections, prostate inflammation, fevers, and high cholesterol, which required additional medications. Yet, he kept up the fiction of rugged good health. He was a young president so robust that he played touch football on the White House lawn. Rumors of potential cognitive decline emerged during the presidency of Ronald Reagan, then the oldest American president. But doctors failed to prove any medical diagnosis, then or since.

President Trump surpassed all past presidents in boasting about the transparency of his administration. In May 2019 he told reporters that "there has never been, ever before, an administration that's been so open and transparent." PolitiFact gave this claim its rare, rock-bottom rating of "Pants on Fire," reserved for only the most flagrant of lies. The fact checkers concluded that "the current administration has been less—not more—transparent than other recent presidents."

Trump failed to release any of his tax returns. He battled in court to deny Congress and New York state prosecutors access to his returns and other financial data. Trump refused to participate in a personal interview with Special Counsel Robert Mueller or to answer questions on obstruction of justice. He evasively responded with versions of "I don't recall" to most written questions about Russian collusion. Trump's press office smashed the record for the number of days without an on-camera briefing. Trump was the first president to force key White House staffers to sign non-disclosure agreements, and he broke President Obama's policy of releasing White House visitor logs. Trump did not provide information on meetings with special interest representatives at his "Southern White House," Mar-a-Lago Golf Club and Resort. On the plus side, Trump provided more media interviews (mostly to friendly outlets) and brief, informal questions and answers than any recent president since Ronald Reagan.

The administration impeded enforcement of the Freedom of Information Act (FOIA), which is the public and the media's best means for prying open in real time the inner workings of a presidency. In an emblematic case, in early 2017, the independent watchdog group Center for Public Integrity filed a FOIA request for documents on potential conflicts of interest by the billionaire Secretary of Commerce Wilbur Ross. Although the law requires government agencies to respond within twenty days to FOIA requests, the Department of Commerce stonewalled the Center, which filed two lawsuits to compel compliance. Only after more than two years of delay and court compulsion did the Department of Commerce finally provide most of the requested information.

In Trump's first year, the Associated Press found that "the federal government censored, withheld or said it couldn't find records sought by citizens, journalists and others more often" than any time in the past decade. In 78 percent of 823,222 record requests, petitioners received either censored files or nothing at all. A study by the nonpartisan Project on Government Oversight (POGO) found that from fiscal 2014 to fiscal 2018, the number of requests received by the Pentagon decreased by about 7 percent, but the amount of information withheld increased by 16 percent, and the backlog of requests reached 11,391—the highest in a decade. The Defense Department shut down the release of information on matters such as non-classified military operations and civilian casualties.

In 2019, Attorney General William Barr challenged the fundamentals of transparency by disparaging public access through FOIA. "Congress has happily created a regime that allows the public to seek whatever documents it wants from the Executive Branch at the same time that individual congressional committees spend their days trying to publicize the Executive's internal decisional process," he said. This "process cannot function properly if it is public, nor is it productive to have our government devoting enormous resources to squabbling about what becomes public and when, rather than doing the work of the people."

While Trump did not imitate Bush in enlarging the classification of documents, he selectively classified and declassified politically sensitive information. Trump did not reveal readouts of calls or meetings with President Putin. He classified the notification sent to Congress under the post-Watergate War Powers Act following the assassination of Iran's general Qassem Soleimani. Conversely, he has declassified documents about the origins of the Russia investigation of his campaign that supposedly support his claim of an improper inquiry.

The eventual scrutiny of Trump's presidential records may still not unravel the mysteries of his administration. According to a report by the nonpartisan POGO, "this administration has demonstrated recklessness with our public records and disregard for the laws and norms meant to safeguard them. The president routinely destroyed vital documents, compelling aides to attempt to salvage some with Scotch tape; officials communicated using encrypted apps that delete their messages and made other efforts to skirt public records requirements."

The administration's lack of transparency helped to camouflage Trump's failures on racial justice, climate change, and the COVID-19 pandemic. After the killing of George Floyd by Minneapolis police officers, Trump set up the Presidential Commission on Law Enforcement and the Administration of Justice. However, it failed to include diverse perspectives beyond law enforcement and blocked public access to meetings. "Commission proceedings have been far from transparent," Senior U.S. District Judge John D. Bates found in response to a lawsuit. "Especially in 2020, when racial justice and civil rights issues involving law enforcement have erupted across the nation," he wrote, "one may legitimately question whether it is sound policy to have a group with little diversity of experience examine, behind closed doors, the sensitive issues facing law enforcement and the criminal justice system in America today."

On Inauguration Day 2017, Trump's State Department withdrew its climate action report from its website. His Environmental Protection Agency wiped out its climate change website, and the administration closed NASA's Carbon Monitoring System, which measured greenhouse gas emissions. In the fall of 2018, the National Climate Assessment, scientists' premier four-year analysis of climate change, warned that global warming endangered public safety and economic growth. After failing to pressure scientists into diluting their findings, Trump released the report the day after Thanksgiving to minimize public attention. For months, in 2019, the government delayed the publication of a news advisory on climate change by the United States Geological Survey. It then removed key findings. In July 2019, the Environmental Protection Agency (EPA) abolished its climate change research group. In December 2019, the Federal Emergency Management Agency eliminated from its annual report guidance on the resources for local governments to prepare for the impacts of climate change.

A May 2020 survey of EPA employees found that the political leadership "interferes with, suppresses, or censors the release of scientific information." Later that year, Trump fired the chief scientist at the National Oceanic and Atmospheric Administration (NOAA). He installed a new political staff of climate change skeptics and put in place tight controls over NOAA's communications with the press and the public. The administration delayed for several months critical work on the next Climate Assessment, due in 2022.

During the pandemic year, the Trump administration withheld scientific information about COVID-19. In a March 9, 2020, briefing, Dr. Nancy Messonnier, director of the National Center for Immunization and Respiratory Diseases at the Centers for Disease Control and Prevention (CDC), correctly warned that coronavirus would rapidly spread in the United States. Trump responded by silencing Messonnier and halting the CDC's public briefings for more than two months. He muzzled other top scientists, including Dr. Anthony Fauci, director of the National Institute on Allergies and Infectious Diseases, and Dr. Deborah Birx, the former coordinator of the White House Coronavirus Task Force. Trump fired Dr. Rick Bright, director of the Biomedical Advanced Research and Development Authority, for refusing to push hydroxychloroquine as a cure for COVID, despite a lack of scientific evidence on its effectiveness and safety. Dr. Bright said that the administration puts "politics and cronyism ahead of science."

Behind the scenes, the White House weakened public health recommendations from authorities on its coronavirus task force. It removed a report on the airborne transmission of COVID-19 from the CDC website. It secretly pressured the CDC to downplay the risks of sending children back to school and to declare that non-symptomatic persons did not need to be tested for coronavirus. The administration failed to explain why it ignored twenty-seven of thirty-one recommendations from the Government Accountability Office (GAO) from February to November 2020 on responding to the pandemic. An unusually harsh GAO 364-page report in early February 2021 noted that "the federal government generally lacks consistent and complete COVID-19 data." National "data on the overall volume of testing are incomplete" and the administration "has not issued a publicly available and comprehensive national testing strategy, creating the risk of key stakeholders and the public lacking crucial information." The administration "misreported" many billions of dollars "in pandemic-related contracts and agreements . . . raising accountability and transparency concerns."

After the election, in late 2020, Vice President Mike Pence, President-elect Joe Biden, and Vice President-elect Kamala Harris televised their COVID-19 inoculations to reassure the public about vaccines. Yet, with polls showing great mistrust of vaccination among his followers, Donald Trump and First Lady Melania arranged for secret vaccinations. This secrecy "is terribly destructive," said Dr. Jonathan Reiner, professor of medicine at George Washington University. "Without the president's very visible assent to vaccines, it has just a devastating result on the acceptance of vaccines in people who doubt it right now." This callous secrecy for a simple COVID vaccination symbolizes Trump's disdain for transparency.

In the 2020 election, Trump smothered transparency more completely than any other presidential candidate. He concealed his outlays by outsourcing $759 million in expenditures to American Made Media Consultants LLC. This was a dark-money, shell company created by Trump campaign aides. Unlike regular campaign committees, it was not required to disclose its expenses to the Federal Elections Committee. According to the Center for Responsive Politics, this ploy enabled the Trump campaign "to hide information about the identities of some individuals being paid by the campaign, how much money changed hands and when those payments took place."

Following the 2020 election, Trump's aggressive fund-raising netted more than $200 million, allegedly to support his legal challenges. However, the fine print of his solicitations tells another story. Trump diverted the first 75 percent of every contribution to his leadership PAC, the Save America Political Action Committee, up to $5,000 (the legal limit). Most donors had little knowledge about the arcane campaign finance laws. "Money flowing into Save America could be spent on just about anything, including paying for meals, lodging, or rounds of golf at Trump properties," said Michael Beckel, the research director for Issue One, an independent political reform group, "expenditures that could ultimately help line the pockets of President Trump and his family." Trump also bilked donors of millions of dollars by surreptitiously signing them up for recurring donations instead of a single contribution.

As a candidate and president, Trump failed to transparently address concerns about his health prompted by his age, weight, poor diet, and lack of exercise. During his 2016 campaign, Trump fabricated a doctor's letter that he dictated to his personal physician, Dr. Harold Bornstein. Despite a lack of medical details, the letter said that "if elected, Mr. Trump, I can state unequivocally, will be the healthiest individual ever elected to the presidency."

In 2018, Trump's White House physician, Dr. Ronny Jackson, whom investigators subsequently found to be drunk on the job, issued another dubiously gushing review. He said that Trump had "incredible genes" and "that if he had a healthier diet over the last twenty years, he might live to be two hundred years old." Jackson also upped Trump's height from 6'2" on his driver's license to 6'3," which put him a pound short of obese. "As in the past, there's little evidence that this assessment is not primarily about good publicity—about outcome, not process," said Dr. James Hamblin, a lecturer at the Yale School of Public Health.

In November 2019, President Trump made an unexpected trip to Walter Reed Medical Center, using a "free weekend" to "begin portions of his routine annual physical exam," said Press Secretary Stephanie Grisham. Two days later, Trump's doctor Sean Conley said that it was no spontaneous visit, but a "routine, planned interim checkup," even though it did not appear on the president's schedule and surprised the Walter Reed doctors. In September 2020, *New York Times* journalist Michael Schmidt reported that the vice president was "to be on standby" to become acting president "temporarily if Trump had to undergo a procedure that would have required him to be anesthetized." Pence responded evasively that he did not "recall being told to be on standby." Trump's reason for his visit "remains a mystery," Schmidt concluded.

In 2020, Trump's failure to follow medical protocols turned the White House into a hotspot for the coronavirus infection. When Trump and Melania tested positive for the virus on October 2, 2020, aides helicoptered Trump to Walter Reed. Trump remained hospitalized for three days. Trump's physicians and the White House issued conflicting and vague assessments of his condition. A February 2021 report in the *New York Times* said that according to people familiar with his condition, Trump's COVID case was more severe than his doctors let on at the time. Trump had "extremely depressed blood oxygen levels at one point and a lung problem associated with pneumonia caused by the coronavirus," and before his hospitalization, "officials believed he would need to be put on a ventilator."

Every modern dictatorship has controlled access to information. The Bolsheviks, who took over the Russian government in 1917, destroyed pre-revolutionary books and journals. They registered typewriters to censor subversive writings and suppressed research in so-called bourgeois science. Adolf Hitler's stormtroopers raided libraries and bookstores. They marched through the nighttime streets by torchlight and tossed the books into huge bonfires. Although our Framers underscored this danger to democracy, America has relied too long on precedent and presidential character to preserve transparency.

### THE FIX: TIGHTEN FOIA AND RULES FOR CLASSIFICATION, ESTABLISH A TRANSPARENCY OMBUDSMAN, AND REQUIRE THE RELEASE OF FINANCIAL AND HEALTH INFORMATION

The Freedom of Information Improvement Act of 2016 introduced significant reforms, but it failed to fully curb abuses in enforcing the law. Congress should allocate funding for every agency, specifically designated for FOIA compliance, and require compliance training for agency officials. The Federation of American Scientists noted that without "new resources for implementation," and in the face of rising demand, "it is unclear how much improvement the FOIA Improvement Act can be expected to generate for the average requester." Congress should authorize inspectors general for federal agencies to review FOIA compliance. They should be empowered to recommend reforms. Provisions should be made for awarding attorney fees and litigation costs to prevailing parties in FOIA litigation.

The late Supreme Court Justice Potter Stewart, an appointee of President Dwight Eisenhower, said that "moral, political, and practical considerations would dictate that a very first principle of . . . wisdom would be an insistence upon avoiding secrecy for its own sake. For when everything is classified, nothing is classified, and the system becomes one to be disregarded by the cynical or the careless, and to be manipulated by those intent on self-protection or self-promotion." Under current law, the standards for classification are so broad and discretionary that "individual classification decisions are apt to be shaped by extraneous factors, including bureaucratic self-interest and public controversy," according to Steven Aftergood, director of the Project on Government Secrecy at the Federation of American Scientists.

Reform would include making public access, not classification, the default option for all agency documents, and would streamline appeals for declassification. A classification ombudsman should be assigned to each agency to monitor over-classification. Training for over-classification should be improved and agency officials should be rewarded, not punished, for good faith efforts at making information available to the public. An independent commission should review classification practices and make recommendations for a government-wide declassification strategy, for upgrading resources, and for quickly and efficiently sharing information on decisions that cut across agency lines. White House and agency documents of historical importance need to be promptly set aside to guarantee their preservation and eventual access.

New laws should require the release of health and financial information by candidates and presidents. They should mandate publication of contacts with the president, including White House visitor logs, with an exception based only on national security. They should eliminate dark-money funding of campaigns and establish a transparency ombudsman for the federal government that would evaluate all disclosed information. The ombudsman would generally monitor transparency issues across the government and disclose transgressions to Congress and the public.

# A Militarized Nation

## *Separating the Military from Politics*

> You know how impossible it is, in short, to have a free
> nation if it is a military nation and under military orders.
>
> —President Woodrow Wilson, 1919

$\mathcal{O}$n March 3, 1991, four Los Angeles police officers outraged the nation when a bystander filmed them brutally beating black motorist Rodney King. They had arrested him for drunk driving after a high-speed chase. The beating afflicted King with skull fractures, broken bones and teeth, and permanent brain damage. More than thirteen months later, after a change of venue from racially mixed Los Angeles, prosecutors tried the officers in predominantly white Simi Valley City. The jury of nine whites, one Latino, one Asian American, and one biracial person acquitted three officers of all charges and failed to reach a verdict on the fourth defendant. Within hours of the verdict, which many black residents believed reflected a pattern of racial discrimination and neglect, a violent six-day riot erupted in Los Angeles. The riot left sixty-three people dead and 2,383 injured. Estimated property damage exceeded $1 billion.

As rioting raged in Los Angeles, then Attorney General William Barr told President George H. W. Bush that he could dispatch federal troops to restore order. Bush responded that he preferred to rely on state and local forces. "Let's not try to resort to regular military right now," he said. Bush finally agreed to send in federal troops only in response to an urgent request from Governor Pete Wilson and Los Angeles Mayor Tom Bradley. They said that state and local forces could not control the violence. President Bush told the nation that "at the request of the Governor and the Mayor, I have committed these troops to help restore order." He said he felt "anger" and "pain" after hearing about the acquittal of the police officers and recognized the failed response of the criminal justice system. He added, "We must allow our diversity to bring us together and not drive us apart. . . . We must build a future where empty rage gives way to hope, where poverty and despair give way to opportunity." However, he insisted that "what is going on in L.A. must and will stop. As your president, I guarantee you this violence will end."

This was the last time before the administration of Donald Trump that a president summoned federal military forces to assume responsibility for enforcing domestic law and order. America's founders had so feared the threat to liberty from the military that they hesitated to authorize a standing army in the Constitution. Instead, they hoped to rely on a well-regulated militia that would later become the National Guard to defend the nation. However, under pressure from immediate enemies—the Indian nations and the colonial powers of Europe—they authorized Congress to "raise and support Armies." However, lawmakers had to renew appropriations every two years. James Madison warned, "A standing military force, with an overgrown Executive will not long be safe companions to liberty. The means of defence [*sic*] against foreign danger, have been always the instruments of tyranny at home."

To ensure the readiness of a citizen militia, the first Congress adopted, and the states ratified, the Second Amendment. It reads, "A well regulated Militia, being necessary to the security of a free State, the right of the people to keep and bear Arms, shall not be infringed." In recent years, the gun lobby and the U.S. Supreme Court have interpreted the Second Amendment to codify an individual right to bear arms and rise up in armed rebellion against an allegedly unjust government. Not a single figure involved in drafting, enacting, or ratifying the amendment suggested such an interpretation. The Framers focused on the militia— an organized, controlled, and regulated force—not on privately armed citizens. James Madison, the author of the amendment, and members of the first Congress, rejected proposals to specify a private right to keep and bear arms.

The staid, law and order Federalists who adopted the Second Amendment had no intention of justifying an armed, internal rebellion.

On the contrary, President George Washington deployed the militia to quell the Whiskey Rebellion of 1794, an armed uprising of Pennsylvania farmers harmed by an excise tax on whiskey. Any yielding to internal insurrections, Washington said, would "violate the fundamental principle of our Constitution, which enjoins that the will of the majority shall prevail." In 1799, President John Adams called upon militia forces to suppress another internal insurrection, the Fries Rebellion, in which predominantly German American settlers resisted the federal government's new tax on their homes and lands.

In 1807, Congress put the emphatic stamp of law on its fear of internal rebellion with the Insurrection Act. The act established the wide umbrella of "all cases of insurrection, or obstruction to the laws." It said, "where it is lawful for the President of the United States to call forth the militia for the purpose of suppressing such insurrection, or of causing the laws to be duly executed, it shall be lawful for him to employ, for the same purposes, such part of the land or naval force of the United States." Congress passed the act without debate; no commentator at the time raised an objection based on an alleged Second Amendment right to keep and bear private arms as a check on government.

Despite the fear of insurrection, in 1878, Congress adopted an amendment to the Army Appropriations Bill that restricted the use of the military as a "Posse Comitatus" for domestic law enforcement. Although it did not overrule the Insurrection Act, the new law was designed to outlaw the willful use of any part of the armed forces to execute domestic law, not insurrections, unless expressly authorized by "the Constitution or by act of Congress." The act, as amended, applies to the National Guard during federal service.

During the last one hundred years, pre-Trump presidents have deployed federal forces to assume responsibility for domestic law enforcement for limited reasons. As in the 1992 Los Angeles riots, presidents have responded to requests from state and local authorities unable to quell violence without federal military assistance. These officials requested a federal military force, for example, in response to the Detroit race riot in 1967 and the 1968 race riots in Washington, D.C., Chicago, and Baltimore. The amended Insurrection Act (Section 251 of U.S. Code Title 10) authorizes the president to use the military to suppress an insurgency at the request of a state legislature, or the governor.

In 1970, in response to unruly student demonstrations at Kent State University, Governor James A. Rhodes requested the deployment of National Guard troops. What followed was one of the tragedies of modern American history and a warning to future presidents. After a skirmish in which protesters threw stones and troops fired tear gas canisters, some of the guards opened fire. They killed four students and wounded nine others. The President's Commission on Campus Unrest found that "the indiscriminate firing of rifles into a crowd of students and the deaths that followed were unnecessary, unwarranted, and inexcusable."

Presidents have also deployed troops to enforce a federal court order in the face of state resistance. Section 252 of Title 10 empowers the president to deploy the military when he determines "that unlawful obstructions, combinations, or assemblages, or rebellion against the authority of the United States, make it impracticable to enforce the laws of the United States in any State by the ordinary course of judicial proceedings." In 1957, President Dwight Eisenhower sent federal troops to enforce the integration of Central High School in Little Rock, Arkansas, in the face of state resistance to a federal court order. "Federal troops are not being used to relieve the local and state authorities of their primary duty to preserve the peace and order of the community," President Eisenhower emphatically said. "The troops are there, pursuant to law, solely for the purpose of preventing interference with the orders of the court."

In 1962, President John F. Kennedy used federal troops to enforce a court order compelling the University of Mississippi to admit its first black student, James Meredith. Kennedy said regretfully that this deployment "was necessary in this case, but all other avenues and alternatives, including persuasion and conciliation, had been tried and exhausted."

President Trump mobilized the military domestically for purposes quite different from former presidents. In the fall of 2018, Trump warned of an invading caravan of Central American migrants filled with "some very bad people," like MS-13 gang members and Middle Eastern terrorists. Just one week before the 2018 midterm elections, Trump declared that the caravan presented a "national emergency" and that he would send thousands of National Guard troops to the border. "This is an invasion of our Country and our Military is waiting for you!" Trump tweeted. This was not the first time that presidents had sent National Guard forces to the border, but they had done so in response to requests from state officials. Or they assisted law enforcement in dealing with cross-border drug trafficking, which President Ronald Reagan had officially designated as a "national security" emergency and which is authorized under law as part of the "war on drugs." In Trump's case, the supposed "national emergency" was a fabricated sham. The refugee caravan was still a few weeks from the border and consisted mainly of women and children without any terrorists or troubling criminal elements among them.

By deploying troops to the border, Trump hoped to frighten American voters on the eve of the midterm elections. The Democrats, Trump charged, want "open borders" and "want caravans, they like the caravans." "Tomorrow is one week before the election, which is what this is all about," said Fox News Anchor Shepard Smith. "There is no invasion. No one is coming to get you. There is nothing at all to worry about." Former Republican Speaker of the House and presidential candidate Newt Gingrich explained that "Trump understands in the current American political structure, you have to win polarized campaigns."

In the wake of demonstrations that demanded racial justice nationwide in the spring of 2020, Trump warned that if states or cities refused to act forcefully against demonstrators, "then I will deploy the U.S. military and quickly solve the problem for them." He told the governors, "You have to dominate—if you don't dominate, you're wasting your time." The president resurrected a racist slogan from the 1960s, saying, "Any difficulty and we will assume control, but, when the looting starts, the shooting starts."

Trump deployed the military in Washington, D.C., when he mobilized more than five thousand federalized National Guard troops in advance of anticipated protests. Trump summoned the forces not in response to requests from an overwhelmed local government or to enforce federal law as a last resort remedy. Trump instead used the Guard to contain and manipulate politically unwelcome demonstrators.

On June 1, 2020, police officers backed by National Guard troops waded into a crowd of peaceful protestors. As the television footage showed, they used chemical irritants, rubber bullets and batons to scatter demonstrators near the White House. The president then used the cleared path for a photo opportunity. He walked to nearby St. John's

Church, which he did not attend, to hold aloft a Bible that he had not read. National Guard Major Adam DeMarco, an Iraq War combat veteran, found the event that he had witnessed at close hand, "deeply disturbing." He said, "Having served in a combat zone, and understanding how to assess threat environments, at no time did I feel threatened by the protestors or assess them to be violent." DeMarco added, "From my observation, those demonstrators—our fellow American citizens—were engaged in the peaceful expression of their First Amendment rights. Yet they were subjected to an unprovoked escalation and excessive use of force."

General Mark Milley, the nation's leading military commander, who chaired the Joint Chiefs of Staff, walked behind President Trump to the church, clad in full combat fatigues. Milley later apologized for his presence, which appeared to give military sanction to a political event. "I should not have been there," he said. "My presence in that moment and in that environment created a perception of the military involved in domestic politics. . . . We who wear the cloth of our nation come from the people of our nation. And we must hold dear the principle of an apolitical military that is so deeply rooted in the very essence of our Republic." Milley added that he was "outraged" by the killing of George Floyd and that protests speak "to the centuries of injustice toward African Americans." Milley opposed using federal troops to police demonstrations on American streets.

In July 2020, Trump sent unidentified federal forces to suppress the protests in Portland, Oregon, with camouflage gear and combat weapons, making them inseparable from federal troops. The officers had no body cameras and no name tags (to protect them from retaliation, officials said). Video footage shows that any other identifying information was lost in the military camouflage. The Trump administration indicated that the Department of Homeland Security had lawfully enlisted the unidentified officers or troopers to help protect federal property, essentially a mandate without limit. "An interpretation of that authority so broadly seems to undermine all the other careful checks and balances on DHS's power because the officers' power is effectively limitless and all-encompassing," said Garrett Graff, a historian of American policing and national security. Unidentified federal agents peppersprayed and beat Navy veteran Christopher David, breaking two of his bones. David had committed no crimes; he had been calmly watching the protests. The federal forces tear-gassed nonviolent demonstrators, including a peaceful "wall of mothers" and the mayor of Portland. They pulled non-violent people off the streets, away from a federal building, and dragged them into unidentified vehicles.

Before President Trump, presidents have largely kept the military separate from politics. Trump never served in the military. No one in Trump's immediate family served. Not his parents. Not any of his children. During the war in Vietnam, he received a questionable medical deferment for bone spurs. "When we ain't fightin', we should act like sojers," the GI Willie told his sidekick Joe, in one of Bill Mauldin's iconic Willie and Joe cartoons from World War II. Despite never "fightin'," Trump playacted like a "sojer." He wrapped himself in the glory of America's soldiers more than any other president—even the apex commanders such as George Washington, Ulysses Grant, and Dwight Eisenhower, and decorated war heroes like John F. Kennedy and George H. W. Bush. In the process, he crossed the line between the military and politics.

One week after his inauguration as president, Trump witnessed the swearing-in by Vice President Mike Pence of his new Secretary of Defense, retired General James Mattis. The event took place at the Pentagon's Hall of Heroes, which honors every winner of the highest military award, the Congressional Medal of Honor. Trump then used the backdrop of this sacred military space to announce his travel ban on residents of predominantly Muslim nations. Never before had a president used the Hall of Heroes as a political prop. A few days later, Trump used the military backdrop at MacDill Air Force Base to deliver an openly political address to officers and troops. "We had a wonderful election, didn't we?" he said. "And I saw those numbers, and you liked me and I liked you. That's the way it worked." White House officials had the Navy keep the destroyer, the USS *John McCain*, "out of sight" in deference to Trump's clashes with the late Senator, when the president visited Japan in May 2019.

In June 2020, amid the pandemic, Trump summoned army cadets back to West Point to deliver in person a politically slanted graduation address. A video at the Republican National Nominating Convention on August 25, 2020, featured two marines in full dress uniform saluting the president as he walked through the White House. The United States Marine Corps Band provided musical support for a blatantly political event on the White House lawn after Trump returned from treatment for COVID-19 at Walter Reed Medical Center. Trump told the crowd to vote his opponents "into oblivion. Got to get rid of them so bad for our country." He attacked "Sleepy Joe Biden" and said, "We're starting very, very big with the rallies, and with our everything, because we cannot allow our country to become a socialist nation." The crowd responded by chanting, "Four more years."

During the 2020 campaign and its aftermath, Trump used military language to recruit supporters and stoke his grievances. In March 2020, his campaign began to recruit volunteers for the "Army for Trump," which would "mobilize Americans across the country who are committed to fighting to reelect President Trump." The campaign websites called upon supporters to join the "frontlines," with "battle-tested Team Trump operatives," and become the Trump army's "field staff." A Trump fund-raising email in June 2020 said, "The President wants YOU and every other member of our exclusive Trump Army to have something to identify yourselves with, and to let everyone know that you are the President's first line of defense when it comes to fighting off the Liberal MOB." Trump and his surrogates used the words *fight*, *fighting*, or an equivalent hundreds of times in 2020 and 2021, including twenty times in his January 6 rally speech. Military language is of particular significance when it comes from the commander-in-chief of the U.S. armed forces.

President Trump's rhetoric and actions may also have exacerbated a lingering problem of right-wing extremism within the ranks of America's military. A 2019 survey by the *Military Times* found that 36 percent of troops who responded have seen evidence of white supremacist and racist ideologies in the military, a nearly two-thirds rise from 2018, when in the same poll only 22 percent reported seeing such evidence. An NPR survey found that nearly one in five people charged for alleged involvement in the Capitol insurrection appear to have a military history, about double the 9 percent of the U.S. adult population.

As illustrated by the Trump presidency, the hard line that the Framers sought to draw between the military and internal policies and politics is all but erased. The array of laws governing the domestic deployment of the armed forces is archaic, confusing, and contradictory. They impose little restraint on presidential abuse. The militarization of policing is Trump's version of Orwell's "boot in the face" subversion of democracy. Keep a terrified people in line behind the combined conjurer and strongman, cancelling their democratic choice.

## THE FIX: DEFINE LIMITS ON MILITARY DEPLOYMENT, REQUIRE BODYCAMS AND CLEAR ID, REFORM POLICING, TIGHTEN THE LAWS AGAINST POLITICAL ACTIVITY BY THE MILITARY, AND ROOT OUT EXTREMISM

Federal law should clarify the criteria for using the military within the United States. Amendments to the Insurrection Act should distinguish clearly between mobilizing armed forces for domestic law enforcement as opposed to repelling a foreign military or terrorist attack, responding to a natural disaster, suppressing an internal rebellion, or fighting a foreign war. In all but these extreme circumstances, any deployment of military forces should be a policy of last resort. Authority should be limited to requests from state or local officials unable to contain lawlessness with their own resources and the enforcement of federal law or court orders after exhausting all other alternatives. The amendments should require congressional notification and approval for any deployment beyond forty-eight hours and provide for expedited judicial review.

When an administration deploys military personnel or federal law enforcement agents to localities, they should wear body cameras. They should display clearly legible organization badges and identification numbers, in lieu of name tags. The officers should be prohibited from arrests or detentions without probable cause of specific crimes. They should be subject to strict liability standards for inflicting wrongful harm. Congress should enact the reforms of policing embodied in the George Floyd Justice in Policing Act.

Congress should tighten prohibitions against partisan political activity by the military by specifying examples, such as providing support through bands and parades or even becoming a visible, standby presence at political events. Congress should make it unlawful for a president to order military personnel, directly or indirectly, to take part in any partisan political activity, such as President Trump's photo op at St. John's Church.

In February 2021, new Defense Secretary Lloyd J. Austin ordered a sixty-day "stand down," which reserved time for the military for discussions of extremism within their ranks. More needs to be done. Each branch of the armed forces should establish an internal law enforcement task force dedicated to monitoring and rooting out extremist networks of troops. The military should practice prevention by screening for extremist views at the point of recruitment and requiring anti-extremism training. Education in military academies should emphasize the values of tolerance, diversity, and inclusion, as well as patriotism. Education should include means to detect and deal with dangerous conspiracy theories, anti-Semitism, and racism, without foreclosing freedom of expression.

# Voter Suppression

*Restoring the Franchise*

Voting is not only our right—it is our power.

—Human rights activist Loung Ung, 2011

*W*illiam Fogg filed the first voting rights lawsuit in American history, not in the aftermath of post–Civil War Reconstruction, but in 1835. Fogg was a voter-qualified, free black citizen of Pennsylvania, a commonwealth founded on the premise that "all men are born equally free and independent." He charged that election officials had barred him from his polling place just because he looked black. An adverse decision by the Pennsylvania Supreme Court, in effect, wrote black people out of American democracy. It ignored the colorblind state constitution and found that "no coloured race was party to our social compact," and that there was no basis on which "to raise this depressed race to the level of the white one." The court held out some hope for future generations, when black people might turn white: a black man's "blood, however, may become so diluted in successive descents to lose its distinctive character; and, then, both policy and justice require that previous disabilities should cease."

Plaintiff Fogg pleaded his case in state, not federal court, because of a loophole in the U.S. Constitution. America's Framers did not inscribe a right to vote in the original Constitution or the Bill of Rights. Despite this omission, constitutional delegates recognized that popular consent grounded their democratic republic. In James Madison's words, government "derives all its powers directly or indirectly from the great body of the people, and is administered by persons holding their offices . . . for a limited period, or during good behavior."

However, the Framers believed in limiting the franchise to male property holders, with a "stake in society." No constitutional delegate proposed making suffrage a constitutional right. Neither did any senator or representative when the first Congress debated the Bill of Rights. In dismissing out of hand the idea of "universal suffrage," John Adams said, "I cannot clearly comprehend what is meant by the phrase Universal Suffrage. Is the whole human species to be allowed an equal vote—are all the Women and Children to turn out? are all the parish paupers to come to the Hustings? are all the gaols [*sic*] to be emptied and all the Prisoners to appear? are all the Gypsys and beggars in the town streets and the fields to be assembled?" Adams and other men of influence answered with a resounding no.

Views changed, and Americans gradually embraced an expanded suffrage. Yet, the vote remains embattled today because all subsequent amendments protecting the voting rights of racial minorities, women, and young people—the Fifteenth Amendment on race, the Nineteenth Amendment on sex, and the Twenty-Sixth Amendment on age—are framed negatively. The amendments only specify what states may not do. No amendment conferred an affirmative right to vote on any American.

In the nineteenth century, America made the transition to a "white man's republic." Most states granted suffrage rights to nearly all adult white males regardless of economic status, while disenfranchising people deemed unfit for political life: women, Native Americans, and African Americans. Racial and gender exclusions guarded against voter fraud, leaders at the time falsely claimed. These restrictions allegedly prevented unscrupulous politicians from buying the votes of dependent women and ignorant blacks.

New Jersey, for example, in 1807 ended its unique position as the only state in the early republic to authorize voting by women. It also for the first time disenfranchised all nonwhites. An opinion writer in the *Trenton Federalist* praised the new exclusions. It had ended, he wrote, "what has made our elections disagreeable, contentious, and corrupt; all Females and Negroes being now deprived of a vote, who, not being eligible to nor much acquainted with the affairs of government, need not any longer be made use of to answer a party purpose." By 1860, of the thirty-three states then in the union, only five New England states with minimal black populations authorized voting by nonwhites. No state allowed women to vote.

It took a Civil War, passage of postwar Reconstruction laws, and enactment of the Fifteenth Amendment to enfranchise black Americans, north and south. To secure black voting in former Confederate states from violent intimidation by white vigilante groups like the Ku Klux Klan and the White League, Congress passed legislation that empowered the federal government to bypass state courts and prosecute individuals for violations of the law. The laws authorized the use of federal troops where state and local officials could not maintain the peace.

Despite enforcement efforts, white violence and intimidation of black voters continued, while the northern public wearied of enforcement. Testimony before Congress documented how white supremacist Democrats seeking to "redeem" southern states from Reconstruction ruthlessly suppressed black voting. In the majority-black Barbour County, Alabama, black voters had been electing local Republican officials since the onset of Reconstruction. Then, on Election Day in 1874, a mob of armed whites stormed the county polling place near the town of Eufaula. They shot black voters, killing at least seven, wounding some seventy more, and driving others from the polls. The election supervisor, Elias M. Keils, heard the white men shouting, "Kill him, damn him, kill him." But they misfired and killed Keils's sixteen-year-old son, who was standing at his side. The murderers escaped conviction by silencing witnesses. Few blacks dared to vote again in Barbour County, defaulting control of its government to white Democrats.

While many courageous African Americans continued to vote, white terrorist tactics toppled Reconstruction governments. Reconstruction effectively died when Congress failed in 1875 to enact legislation to enforce the Fifteenth Amendment by protecting black voters. "The colored men, who compose the body of the Republican Party, have been made 'peaceful' by the shot-gun of the raiding white leaguer, the bowie-knife of the southern desperado or the whip-lash of the ex-slave master," said Republican Representative Charles Hays of Alabama. If this continues, "Our doom is sealed . . . What we do want is a fair chance to express ourselves at the ballot-box for the men of our choice."

In the 1890s, white supremacists turned to more subtle and effective ways of disenfranchising black people than mob violence. Between

1890 and 1910, every former Confederate state purposely disenfranchised black people by law. The states adopted stringent residency requirements, poll taxes, and literacy tests with discretion for interpretation by white registrars. Even earlier, Southern states had begun to enact and expand laws depriving criminals and ex-criminals of their right to vote. They often tailored applicable crimes to African American offenders, such as larceny and moral turpitude. "Let's tell the truth if it bursts the bottom of the Universe," said Solomon Saladin, a delegate to Mississippi's Constitutional Convention of 1890. "We came here to exclude the Negro. Nothing short of this will answer." Ben Tillman, who served as governor and senator from South Carolina, said in 1909, "We reorganized the Democratic Party with one plank, and one plank only—namely, that this is a White man's country, and the White men must govern it."

As advocates of black suffrage had warned, court rulings immunized these laws from the Fifteenth Amendment because they did not explicitly target voters "on account of race." It did not matter that in practice they deprived black electors of their right to vote with surgical precision. A study of turnout in the eleven former Confederate states found that black participation in presidential elections tumbled from an average of 61 percent in 1880 to but 2 percent in 1912.

The Nineteenth Amendment to the Constitution in 1920 granted women the right to vote. The Voting Rights Act of 1965 and subsequent amendments enfranchised many millions of nonwhite minorities. It eliminated literacy tests and authorized federal officials to register voters and monitor elections. Under the act, Department of Justice attorneys and private parties could mount legal challenges to discriminatory voting laws and practices. The act required certain states and jurisdictions with a history of voter discrimination to preclear as nondiscriminatory any changes in electoral laws or regulations with the U.S. Department of Justice. Alternatively, a covered state or locality could apply to the Federal District Court of D.C. for a declaratory ruling with the burden of proof on jurisdiction.

Native Americans, like other minorities, struggled for voting rights. The Indian Citizenship Act of 1924 conferred federal citizenship and, in principle, the right to vote for all Indians in the United States. However, seven states with substantial Indian populations still effectively prohibited them from voting. They disenfranchised Indians, for example, by denying the franchise to those who maintained their tribal affiliations, lived on reservations, or were considered under the "guardianship" of government. Some states excluded from voting "Indians not taxed," mimicking a clause of the original Constitution that excluded these persons from the U.S. Census count.

Finally, in the 1950s, states repealed legal prohibitions on Indian voting. Even in the post-repeal era, Indian voting rights remained precarious as states used mechanisms such as at-large election systems and gerrymandered redistricting plans to limit the impact of the Indian vote, prompting litigation under the Voting Rights Act of 1965 and its amendments. In North Dakota, after Democrat Heidi Heitkamp was elected senator by three thousand votes in 2012, the Republican legislature required proof of a street address as a prerequisite for voting. The law placed a disparate burden on the Democratic base of Native American voters, who often live on unnamed roads and depend upon post office boxes for the delivery of mail.

With the passage of the Voting Rights Act, the players and the tactics changed. But the battle remained much the same, with the same rights at stake. Through the middle years of the twentieth century, it was Democrats who restricted the voting of predominantly Republican nonwhites. Since then, with the reversal of racially linked voting, it is the Republicans who benefit from the suppression of minority voters.

Trump said in March 2020 that "the things they had in there were crazy. They had things, levels of voting that if you'd ever agreed to it, you'd never have a Republican elected in this country again." Trump's ally Senator Lindsey Graham of South Carolina said after the 2020 election that "mail-in voting," which fueled high minority voting, "is a nightmare for us." Without changes, "we're never going to win again presidentially." In March 2021, attorneys for Arizona and the Republican Party argued that the U.S. Supreme Court should overturn an appeals court decision striking down restrictive voting measures. "What's the interest of the Arizona RNC in keeping" certain restrictions, asked Justice Amy Comey Barrett. "Because it puts us at a competitive disadvantage relative to Democrats," Michael Carvin, the GOP's lawyer, responded. "Politics is a zero-sum game," he said. "And every extra vote they get through unlawful interpretation of Section 2 hurts us, it's the difference between winning an election fifty to forty-nine and losing an election fifty-one to fifty."

Such strategic thinking about a restricted franchise that empowers Republicans is not new. In 1980, during the campaign to elect Ronald Reagan, GOP strategist Paul Weyrich, a founder of the contemporary conservative movement, criticized what he called the "goo-goo syndrome—good government. They want everybody to vote," he said. "I don't want everybody to vote. Elections are not won by a majority of people . . . as a matter of fact our leverage in the elections quite candidly goes up as the voting populace goes down."

In 2013, while commenting on the Republican advantage from low turnout, Scott Tranter of the Republican consulting firm Optimus (which specializes in election analysis) said, "A lot of us are campaign professionals and we want to do everything we can to help our sides. Sometimes we think that's voter ID, sometimes we think that's longer lines, whatever it may be." Ken Emanuelson, a Tea Party leader in Texas, was leading a 2013 meeting dedicated to turning out Republicans. When a black pastor asked him, "What are the Republicans doing to get black people to vote?" Emanuelson responded, "Well, I'm going to be real honest with you. The Republican Party doesn't want black people to vote if they're going to vote nine to one for Democrats." In Wisconsin, then-Republican state senate staffer Todd Allbaugh testified under oath in a 2016 court hearing. He said that at a closed-door meeting, several Republican senators were "giddy" and "politically frothing at the mouth" in anticipation of a photo voter ID law that would restrict the Democratic base vote.

The new voter suppression justifies restrictive measures by reviving the myth of voter fraud. Yet study after study has demonstrated that voter fraud has been vanishingly small in recent elections. An analysis by the National Republican Lawyer's Association aimed at uncovering as much voter fraud as possible found only 332 alleged cases of voter fraud of any kind nationwide from 1997 through 2011, out of many hundreds of millions of ballots cast.

Modern voter suppression takes many forms, such as photo identification requirements, stringent voter purges, and restrictions on early voting, mail-in voting, and registration drives. It includes poll closings in minority communities, and the continued disenfranchisement of former felons. In addition, the political and racial gerrymandering of congressional and state and local legislative districts are aimed at making minority votes less effective. Like the literacy test and the poll tax, these restrictions do not explicitly mention race, but in practice their burden falls most heavily on minorities.

In the 2013 *Shelby v. Holder* case, a U.S. Supreme Court decision of five to four that fell along ideological lines gutted the Voting Rights Act by striking down its pre-clearance requirement. Chief Justice John Roberts's majority opinion said that there was now little difference between covered and uncovered jurisdictions, and that minorities no longer confront the "pervasive," "flagrant," "widespread," and "rampant" discrimination of the 1960s. He failed to consider the more subtle, but still effective discrimination of the new voter wars. In a study of voting rights violations, historian J. Morgan Kousser refuted the Court's claim of minimal recent voting rights violations in covered jurisdictions. Dallas minister Peter Johnson, a civil rights activist since the 1960s, said, "There's nobody that's going to shoot at you if you register to vote today. They aren't going to bomb your church. They aren't going to get you fired from your job. You don't have those kinds of overt, mean-spirited behaviors today that we experienced years ago. . . . They pat you on the back, but there's a knife in that pat."

Six years later, in 2019, another five to four decision along ideological lines barred the federal judiciary from considering gerrymandering cases. Chief Justice John Roberts again wrote the majority opinion. Federal judges "have no license to reallocate political power between the two major political parties," he wrote. The Court wiped out a finding from a three-judge federal district court that North Carolina's congressional redistricting plan violated the U.S. Constitution. In 2016, Republicans won 53 percent of the statewide congressional votes but carried 77 percent of congressional seats (10 of 13). Plaintiffs now must rely on litigation in state, not federal courts.

Donald Trump escalated false charges of voter fraud. After losing the popular vote by 2.9 million votes in 2016, Trump claimed that after erasing illegal votes, he really beat Clinton nationwide. He said that, like the legendary Scottish city of Brigadoon rising from the mist for a single day, "three to five million illegal voters" miraculously appeared from nowhere on Election Day. They all voted for Clinton, and then, like Brigadoon, inexplicably disappeared. He added that if not for the "thousands" of people who were "brought in on buses from neighboring Massachusetts to illegally vote in New Hampshire," he would have won the state's four electoral votes.

A 2018 analysis published in *Electoral Studies* found, "Our empirical results share a common theme: they are inconsistent with fraud allegations made by Trump. The results are, however, consistent with various state-level investigations conducted in the initial months of 2017, all of which have failed to find any evidence of widespread voter fraud in the 2016 General Election." Further evidence showed "no support for the so-called Massachusetts busing theory."

Prior to anyone casting a single vote in 2020, Trump charged that the election would be marred by massive fraud in mail-in ballots. In June 2020, Trump warned that Democrats are "trying to rig the election," which will be "the most corrupt election in the history of our country, and we cannot let that happen." A month later, Trump said that "mail-in voting is going to rig the election" and refused to commit to accepting the results. Five states had used all mail-in voting before 2020, including deep red Utah, with no issues of fraudulent voting.

After the election, Trump rejected Joe Biden's victory in critical swing states. He falsely claimed instead that he really won these states by landslide margins, but that felonious Democrats stole the election through massive voter fraud. He maintained this fiction, even as his own Departments of Homeland Security and Justice affirmed the security and fairness of the election and nearly ninety judges, including eight federal jurists that Trump appointed, decisively rejected allegations of a tainted election.

The good news for voting rights is that attempts to restrict voting can backfire. Minority leaders like former gubernatorial candidate Stacey Abrams in Georgia have used attempted suppression to motivate voters. In 2020, voter turnout climbed to a modern record of 67 percent of eligible voters, compared to 60 percent in 2016. In Georgia, the participation rate increased from 59 percent to 68 percent. Both whites and minorities expanded their turnout in 2020.

Instead of celebrating this demonstration of a dynamic American democracy, the Republicans stepped up their efforts to make voting, the most basic democratic right, more difficult, especially for minorities. In justification, they cited the alleged fraud and "irregularities" that Trump and his enablers falsely promoted. A March 2021 study by the Brennan Center for Justice found that legislators had introduced more than 360 restrictive voting bills in forty-seven states, almost exclusively by Republicans. This represents more than ten times the thirty-five restrictive bills introduced at around the same time in 2020.

In a case study of circular reasoning, Republicans claimed that new restrictions would remedy the loss of voter confidence that they had contrived with false charges of an election that Democrats had stolen from Trump. Although racially neutral on their face, the impact of the new strictures falls disproportionately on Democratic-voting minorities who trail whites in income, education, transportation, and command of English. Studies demonstrate so-called anti-fraud laws do not uniformly increase voter confidence. They do so only for Republicans, while decreasing confidence among Democrats.

These restrictions strengthen the Republicans' ability to govern the nation as a minority party. A Gallup Poll found that "throughout the first quarter of 2021, an average of 49% of U.S. adults identified with the Democratic Party or said they are independents who lean toward the Democratic Party. That compares with 40% who identified as Republicans or Republican leaners." The party's base of older white Christian voters is shrinking. It cannot clone more of these voters, so it attempts to limit participation by the rising Democratic base of racial minorities and young people.

Georgia's Republican election officials insisted that their state's election was secure and fair. Yet the Republican majority in the General Assembly, supported by Republican Governor Brian Kemp, passed a new unnecessary law that would limit voting opportunities. The new act imposes stricter voter identification requirements for absentee balloting and makes it more difficult to apply for, complete, and return such ballots. It shortens the time for holding runoff elections. It shifts the power to supervise elections to the Republican legislature by removing the secretary of state from chairing the state Board of Elections and authorizing the legislature to appoint members of the board. It further empowers the state Board of Elections to have sweeping jurisdiction over county elections boards, including the authority to suspend local officials, for example, in heavily minority and Democratic Fulton County. The state of Georgia even made it a crime to offer water or food to voters waiting in lines at the polls. The act expands some opportunities for early voting in general elections, but the impact will be felt primarily in small rural counties, not in diverse urban areas.

The Republican caucus in the Georgia State Senate claimed that "we have heard the calls of millions of Georgians who have raised deep and heartfelt concerns that state law has been violated and our election process abused. We will fix this." Alice O'Lenick, a Republican member of the Gwinnett County Board of Elections in suburban Atlanta, more candidly said, "They've got to change the major parts of them [voter laws] so that we at least have a shot at winning."

In Iowa, a state Trump won in 2020, Republican legislators and the governor nonetheless imposed new restrictions on voting. The new legislation reduces early voting days from twenty-nine to twenty days. It closes polling places an hour earlier on Election Day, at 8 p.m. instead of 9 p.m. It bans officials from sending out absentee ballot applications without a voter first requesting one and requires that ballots must be received before the polls close on Election Day. Previously, ballots could be received by the Monday after the election if they were postmarked by the day before the election.

Other states have adopted or are considering restrictive legislation. In Pennsylvania, Republicans who control the General Assembly have introduced a photo voter identification law and a repeal of the state's bipartisan law authorizing no-excuse absentee voting. Pennsylvania's Democratic governor, Tom Wolf, would surely veto any such measures, as would Democratic governors in the other swing states of Michigan and Wisconsin. "Voter confidence" will likely become an issue in the 2022 election, as the Republicans attempt to win back these governorships. Democrats are hoping to reduce the GOP's advantage in state legislatures.

Nationally, Florida Republican Senator Rick Scott has introduced legislation for a federal photo voter identification requirement. He claimed, "This election has shown we need major reforms to our election systems, including Voter ID laws across the nation, to protect against fraud and rebuild the American people's trust in fair outcomes." Legislation that Scott filed would further limit the time for requesting absentee ballots, overriding state laws that authorize the counting of ballots postmarked but not received by Election Day.

At a February 2014 dinner held by the Harris County Republican Party, conservative Republican Senator Rand Paul of Kentucky advised that rather than restricting the votes of minorities, Republicans should reach out to these voters. "What I do believe is Texas is going to be a Democrat state within ten years if we don't change," he said. "That means we evolve, it doesn't mean we give up on what we believe in, but it means we have to be a welcoming party."

Republicans have yet to heed his advice. Two eighteenth-century institutions, the Senate and the Electoral College, both bolster the GOP's quest to govern from the minority. America's Framers allotted two senators to each state, for pragmatic, not principled reasons. James Madison argued that any departure from proportional representation was "evidently unjust" and "shocks too much the ideas of justice and every human feeling." However, to win ratification of their handiwork by small states, delegates agreed to the "Great Compromise," which established proportional representation for the U.S. House and "equality" for states in the Senate.

The imbalance in Senate representation that Madison decried is much more glaring now than it was in his time. In 1790, the free population of the largest state was 5.7 times that of the smallest state. In 2020, California had 68 times the population of Wyoming, the least populated state. Chief Justice Earl Warren wrote in for the majority in the iconic 1964 one-person, one-voter apportionment decision, *Reynolds v. Sims*, "legislators represent people, not trees or acres. Legislators are elected by voters, not farms or cities or economic interests."

The consequences of the Senate's imbalance are profound. The Senate has become the graveyard of democracy. Senators who come mainly from sparsely populated and unrepresentative states kill laws without regard to support from the American people. Thus, Mitch McConnell, during his years as Republican leader, earned his nickname "The Grim Reaper." The filibuster rule that allows only forty-one senators to block consideration of most bills strengthens minority rule. In this age of mobility, most Americans regard themselves as citizens of the nation, not of a state. Most of the issues before Congress, such as immigration, health care, taxes, gun control, infrastructure, and climate change, are national and not local.

The Senate's lack of population balance infects the Electoral College, because each state receives votes for each of its two senators, plus the number of seats it holds in the House. Each state is guaranteed at least three electoral college votes, even though by population states like Wyoming should have only one. California, which has fifty-five electoral votes, should have sixty-five, per population. In two elections during the last twenty years, 2000 and 2016, the popular vote winner—both Democrats—lost the presidency. Before 2000, the Electoral College and the popular vote had not diverged since 1888. In the last eight elections, Republicans won the popular vote for president only once, in 2004. Even in 2020, when Democrat Joe Biden won nationally by about seven million votes, he barely carried the four swing states of Arizona, Georgia, Nevada, and Wisconsin by less than eighty thousand votes combined.

The 220-year-old battle over the franchise will not end anytime soon. Efforts to restrict voting will continue through the midterm elections of 2022 and the presidential election of 2024. Federal countermeasures are needed.

## THE FIX: NEW VOTING LAWS, SENATE REFORM, AND ADVOCACY FOR THE CONSTITUTIONAL RIGHT TO VOTE

Reforms should both curb voter restrictions and expand opportunities for registration and voting. The omnibus For the People Act of 2021 (H.R. 1) that has passed the U.S. House would transform American elections through needed democratic reforms. It mandates automatic registration when persons obtain or renew driver's licenses or apply for social services. It requires states to enable citizens to register on the same day that they vote at the polls. The bill restricts the purging of citizens from the registration rolls, provides an alternative to photo voter ID laws, makes it a federal crime to impede registration or voting, and restores federal voting rights to ex-felons. It compels all jurisdictions to maintain a paper voting trail, and to offer at least two weeks of early voting. The bill expands opportunities for voting by mail, bans partisan gerrymandering, and requires states to redistrict congressional seats through independent commissions. It protects elections from hacking and disinformation campaigns.

Also needed is a new voting rights act that restores the preclearance of voting changes for states with a recent history of voter discrimination. The fortified law should require transparent explanations for any changes in voting laws and regulations and ease the standards for preliminary injunctions where immediate relief is needed. It should guarantee timely notice of changes in polling locations and prohibit the presence of law enforcement or armed personnel at polling places. It should include a list of non-photo identifications such as utility bills, bank statements, and social security cards that authorize persons to vote in federal elections.

Congress has ample authority for these reforms. Article I, Section 4, Clause 1 of the Constitution (known as the Elections Clause) provides that the states will prescribe the "Times, Places and Manner" of congressional elections, but that Congress may "make or alter" the states' regulations at any time, except as to the places of choosing senators. Since congressional elections in every state are held at the same time and place as presidential elections, federal law would cover both elections. Furthermore, Congress has broad authority to prohibit discriminatory practices in all federal, state, and local elections.

Senate reform, which also rebalances the Electoral College, is challenging but possible. Article V of the Constitution, which requires the consent of each state, prohibits any change in the two-seat-per-state rule. However, Congress and the states could adopt a constitutional amendment that abolishes the existing Senate and replaces it with a renamed upper chamber. The reconstituted body should be roughly based on population: for example, with representation ranging from one to eight for each state in the one-hundred-member chamber.

This change would reduce the Senate's skewed representation, while maintaining meaningful representation for small states, which are guaranteed at least one seat. Americans have reformed the Senate before. In 1913, the Seventeenth Amendment shifted the voting for senators from state legislators to the people. Without abolishing the Electoral College, reform of the Senate would reduce its population imbalance by increasing the number of votes for underrepresented large states and reducing the number of votes for overrepresented small states. This rebalancing would compel candidates to campaign nationally, not just in contested swing states. It would bring the Electoral College result much closer to the ideal of government by the consent of the governed.

It is long past time to enshrine a right to vote in the federal Constitution, which is already part of most state constitutions. Like the amendment to reform the Senate, it will be difficult to obtain the assent of two-thirds of both chambers of Congress and three-quarters of the states. This does not mean, however, that advocates should stop pushing for these vital reforms.

# Postelection Obstruction

## *Reforming Presidential Transitions*

> The national interest requires that such transitions in
> the office of President be accomplished so as to assure
> continuity in the faithful execution of the laws and in the
> conduct of the affairs of the Federal Government, both
> domestic and foreign. Any disruption . . . could produce
> results detrimental to the safety and well-being of the
> United States and its people.

> —Preamble to the Presidential Transition Act of 1963

*W*ith the economy in shambles, voters dismissed the incumbent
Republican president and elected his Democratic rival. There was no
love lost between the two men, who clashed in their policies, partisan
goals, and temperaments. The outgoing president said that the national
crisis resulted from circumstances beyond his control. He believed that
he rated top marks for his response. He insisted that the president-elect
should back his policies and issue an optimistic public statement.

The president-elect demurred; he would not endorse failed policies
that voters had repudiated or deceive the country with false hope. He
wrote that there was a "divergence of opinion between us" in assessing the problems of the time and that "commitments to any particular
polic[ies] . . . are . . . indeed impossible." An influential aide noted that
the president-elect would not engage in "hornswoggling the country
with optimistic statements which everyone knew weren't justified." Another aide said that the new president "had his own plans of an entirely
different character." Until Inauguration Day, the incumbent would bear
responsibility for the nation's woes. A prominent columnist warned of a
breakdown in governance: "The President is virtually without influence.

The President-elect is without authority, so power is divided among the leaders of factions, no one of whom is strong enough to govern, though almost any one of them is strong enough to stop every one else from governing."

This ill-fated transition took place in 1932–1933 between outgoing Republican president Herbert Hoover and president-elect Franklin Roosevelt. It lasted for an agonizing four months. Only in 1936 did the so-called lame duck amendment to the Constitution move the inauguration up from March 4 to January 20. A transition of party power in the White House was not tested again for another twenty years. In 1952, Republican Dwight Eisenhower defeated Adlai Stevenson after the incumbent Democratic President Harry Truman declined to run again.

Much had changed between 1932 and 1952. Years of prosperity had followed the end of the Great Depression and World War II. The federal budget had grown from 7 percent to 19 percent of the nation's Gross Domestic Product. The government now administered vast new programs like Social Security, and it regulated financial markets and labor relations. The United States moved from isolation to worldwide leadership during the Cold War with the Soviet Union. It was fighting a bitterly unpopular hot war in far-off Korea. The Truman administration had established an "invisible government" hidden from public view. Both the United States and the Soviet Union had atomic weapons.

The outgoing president's approach to the transition had changed as well. The day after the election, when Eisenhower's victory became apparent, Truman wrote, "The people of the United States have elected Gen. Dwight D. Eisenhower as their President. In our democracy, this is the way we decide who should govern us. I accept the decision as representing the will of the people, and I shall give my support to the Government they have selected. I ask all my fellow citizens to do the same." He added, "I stand ready to do all that lies within my power to facilitate the orderly transfer of the business of the executive branch of the Government to the new administration." He offered Eisenhower a meeting with the director of the Bureau of the Budget and pledged "to cooperate with respect to other matters relating to the transition to a new administration." Truman invited Eisenhower to the White House, "in order that it may be plain to the whole world that our people are united in the struggle for freedom."

The next transition followed the tight, controversial election of 1960. The result that outgoing president Dwight Eisenhower had dreaded emerged the day after the election, when his vice president, Richard Nixon, conceded to Democrat John F. Kennedy. "All that I've been trying to do for eight years has gone down the drain," Eisenhower told his son. "I might as well just have been having fun." Nevertheless, Eisenhower sent a telegram of congratulations to Kennedy and promptly initiated the transition process. He met with senior officials and instructed them to cooperate with representatives of the incoming administration. He sent a lengthy telegram to Kennedy, promising personal assistance in the transition. Historian John T. Shaw wrote that "Eisenhower had prepared an elaborate process to turn power over to his successor and ordered it to commence." The day before his inauguration, Kennedy publicly praised Eisenhower and his officials. "I don't think there is anything we asked for they haven't done," he said.

The transition continued unabated, although some Republicans, without Nixon's public imprimatur, charged fraud. They demanded recounts or filed lawsuits challenging the results in eleven states. Ironically, the only consequential lawsuit or recount favored Kennedy in the new state of Hawaii. Although Kennedy did not need Hawaii's three votes for an Electoral College majority, a recount turned a 141-vote victory by Nixon into a Kennedy win by 115 votes.

In 1963, Congress formalized the transition process through the Presidential Transition Act. The act had two purposes: to facilitate a prompt and smooth transition and to reduce the need to raise private money for a public responsibility. Democratic Representative Dante Fascell of Florida said during debates on the bill that "it just does not seem proper and necessary to have [the president- and vice president-elect] going around begging for money to pay for the cost of what ought to be legitimate costs of Government."

Fascell explained that "rather than leave this important matter to the discretion or whim of the individuals concerned, it would seem wisdom to guard against the dangers of noncooperation, remote as they may be." Democratic Representative Neil Staebler of Michigan added, "We need to institutionalize the period of changeover because in our age of persistent international and domestic problems we cannot risk discontinuity or disruption in the affairs of government." Republican Representative Clarence J. Brown of Ohio noted that the bill had "bipartisan support" with "little or no opposition." President Kennedy endorsed and signed the bill, saying, it "will go a long way to improve the political climate."

Contrary to common belief, by virtue of this act, as amended, the official transition begins during the campaign, not after the election. The act requires the heads of federal agencies to appoint senior career officials in early May of the election year to oversee transition activities. These officials must prepare a succession plan no later than September 15. Prior to October 1, the president must further negotiate with each eligible candidate a Memorandum of Understanding that at a minimum specifies "the conditions of access to employees, facilities, and documents of agencies by transition staff." Final briefing materials are due no later than November 1.

The postelection transition begins when the administrator of the General Services Administration (GSA) ascertains "the apparent successful candidates for the office of President and Vice President." The administrator then provides funding, office space, office equipment, and communications services to the incoming president. The statute authorizes funding for coordination with the outgoing administration on high-priority information. As soon as possible after the election, the outgoing administration should provide its successors with "a detailed classified, compartmented summary . . . of specific operational threats to national security; major military or covert operations; and pending decisions on possible uses of military force."

This transition process has worked well. The presidential election of 2016, for example, was a bitter and close competition, with fewer than 90,000 votes in three swing states electing Donald Trump, who lost the popular vote. But the Democrat candidate, Hillary Clinton, conceded defeat the day after the election. President Barack Obama invited Donald Trump to the White House. He immediately began the transition and cooperated with the Trump team throughout the process. In his inaugural address, Trump said, "Every four years, we gather on these steps to carry out the orderly and peaceful transfer of power, and we are grateful to President Obama and First Lady Michelle Obama for their gracious aid throughout this transition. They have been magnificent." These were the last kind words that Trump would have for Obama.

Only two notable exceptions have impeded effective transitions since the 1963 act was passed, one inevitable and the other preventable.

The unavoidable exception followed the disputed presidential election of 2000 between Democrat Al Gore and Republican challenger George W. Bush. The outcome turned on a few hundred votes out of some six million cast in the decisive state of Florida. No apparent winner emerged until December 12, when the U.S. Supreme Court cut off a recount with Bush leading by a final 537 votes. The 9/11 Commission concluded that the shortened transition had hindered the new administration's preparation for terrorist attacks.

Despite good reasons for delaying ascertainment of the 2000 winner, the administrator of the GSA provided misleading explanations. In a press advisory on November 9, 2000, the GSA said that the losing candidate would have to concede before it could determine the "apparent successful candidate." It later dropped the concession requirement and said that the electoral dispute, not a failure to concede, made the result "unclear and unapparent."

The avoidable exception occurred after the 2020 election. On November 7, four days after Election Day, the cable news networks, the Associated Press, and broadcast news divisions unanimously called the election for Joe Biden and Kamala Harris. Yet Emily Murphy, President Trump's political appointee to head the GSA, refused to ascertain a winner. She still delayed ascertainment after election officials, including Republicans, from all contested states declared the election clean. She waited until November 23, more than two weeks after Biden's apparent win.

Murphy disingenuously claimed that "ascertain means to determine with certainty." She contradicted the letter of the law that set the low bar of ascertaining only an "apparent," not a certain winner. She further claimed to have relied on "precedent from prior elections involving legal challenges and incomplete counts." However, in each previous election, the GSA administrator had begun the formal transition as soon as the media outlets declared a winner. The special circumstances of 2000 had no analog in 2020 and provided no precedent for her delay.

Trump's political appointees both delayed and disrupted the transition. On December 17, 2020, Trump's acting secretary of defense Chris Miller announced a "mutually agreed upon" arrangement with the Biden team to delay briefings for more than two weeks, until after the holidays. This was false. "There was no mutually agreed upon holiday break," Yohannes Abraham, a spokesman for Biden's transition team told reporters. "We believe it's important," he said, that the briefings continue, "as there is no time to spare."

On December 28, the usually circumspect Biden accused political appointees in Defense and the Office of Management and Budget of continuing obstruction. "My team needs a clear picture of our force posture around the world and our operations to deter our enemies," Biden said. "We need full visibility into the budget planning underway at the Defense Department and other agencies in order to avoid any window of confusion or catch-up that our adversaries may try to exploit."

On January 3, 2021, all ten living former secretaries of defense, Republican and Democrat, wrote an open letter that decried Trump's obstruction of the transition, which is "a crucial part of the successful transfer of power." At "a time when U.S. forces are engaged in active operations around the world, it is all the more imperative that the transition at the Defense Department be carried out fully, cooperatively and transparently," they said. The administration must avoid any action that would "hinder the success of the new team." They should facilitate the tradition "as so many generations of Americans have done before them. This final action is in keeping with the highest traditions and professionalism of the U.S. armed forces, and the history of democratic transition in our great country."

An analysis that *Politico* published on Inauguration Day concluded that Trump's political appointees had "blocked members of President Joe Biden's incoming administration from gaining access to critical information about current operations, including the troop drawdown in Afghanistan, upcoming special operations missions in Africa and the COVID-19 vaccine distribution program." Only after the transition ended and he assumed office did President Biden learn that the "vaccine program is in worse shape than we anticipated or expected." A Gallup Poll taken in late January found that 66 percent of respondents were dissatisfied with Trump's rollout of vaccines.

Such delays and obstruction in the transition are a "five-alarm fire" for the nation, said Max Stier, director of the Center for Presidential Transition. "What's at stake," in the transition, he said, "really, is our security, our safety. And with the world we're in today, with the economic challenges that are incredibly severe, we have a lot that we should be worried about." He notes that more than one hundred major federal agencies "have different urgent issues that they're addressing, and problems and decisions that would have to be made right away following the inauguration." A thwarted transition also impedes the placement of the new president's team of some four thousand appointed positions. "Having your team on the field, real time, is really fundamental," Stier said. And critical to America's national security is the president-elect's access to the President's Daily Intelligence Brief and other classified information.

Stier points out that it is much more damaging to delay a transition than to redirect a transition once begun. The initiation of the transition process does not prevent an apparently losing candidate from seeking redress in the courts. A new team needs "to be prepared to run our country, and if President Trump somehow manages to change that election outcome, then there's no harm there. But there is real harm if they don't get these resources."

There is bipartisan concern about deficiencies in presidential transitions. "This year's transition highlights a number of significant shortcomings in the governing statute for transitions, and I think this is something that we all need to look at," said Republican Representative Jody Hice of Georgia, the ranking member of the Oversight and Reform Subcommittee, during a December 2020 hearing on transition reform. Democratic Representative Gerry Connolly, the subcommittee chair, agreed. "I do think that Mr. Hice and I and others on the subcommittee, on the full committee, can try to find common ground, though, in dealing with some of the crevices that have been exposed" in the transition process, he said.

## THE FIX: REFORM THE
## PRESIDENTIAL TRANSITION ACT

The problem with presidential transitions is that a political appointee decides when to begin the transition and the outgoing administration controls the process, with few constraints. The administrator of the General Services Administration should not ascertain the outcome of presidential elections. "Something is wrong with the system where the responsibility for declaring the winner of a presidential election seems to devolve upon the General Services Administration—it's the Government's landlord. They buy furniture," said Jim Talent, a former Republican senator from Missouri.

Congress should amend the Presidential Transition Act to establish a bipartisan panel that ascertains an apparent winner and oversees the transition. Minnesota offers a model for this reform. Republican and Democrat leaders each select a panelist to resolve electoral disputes. By mutual agreement, the two partisan appointees pick a third and final member. For the federal transition panel, a vote of any two members on ascertainment would begin the transition process. The amended legislation should clarify that "apparent" does not mean certainty. It should stipulate that ascertainment does not require a concession from the apparently losing candidate or the final resolution of all pending litigation. It should require the transition to begin promptly, with an expedited judicial review of challenges to a delayed ascertainment. The lame duck president and his officials should be prohibited from contacting the committee.

Congress should also clarify the responsibilities and duties of outgoing administrations to facilitate transitions. It should provide access to the President's Daily Intelligence Brief by the president-elect. Congress should impose a clear obligation on outgoing administrations to provide information and cooperate with the elected president and his team by a certain date.

# • *13* •

# Rigged If I Lose, Fair If I Win

## *Protecting Election Results*

> The orderly transfer of authority as called for in the Constitution routinely takes place. . . . In the eyes of many in the world, this every-four-year ceremony we accept as normal is nothing less than a miracle.
>
> —President Ronald Reagan, 1981

*W*ith the presidential election approaching in 1800, leaders of the Federalist Party feared that Thomas Jefferson, the impending opposition candidate, would defeat their incumbent president, John Adams. Early in the year, Federalist Senator James Ross used allegations of fraud to concoct a scheme that would bypass the voters and by fiat guarantee Adams a second term. Ross introduced legislation for a "Grand Committee" controlled by the Federalists to assess the "legality or illegality of the votes" cast in each state. The Committee would meet in secret to decide which votes to count, in effect assuming the power to appoint the next president, with no appeal from its decisions.

Federalist leaders "were determined that, if the presidential election could not be carried by fair means, it should by foul," explained historian John Bach McMaster. "Adams's electors might be defeated . . . but the votes of the Jefferson electors should, if possible, be thrown out by Congress." Jefferson's ally, James Madison, warned against this "licentiousness in constructive perversions of the Constitution." Differences between the two chambers of Congress and public outrage eventually killed the bill. In the spring of 1800, Adams met Jefferson and promised to be a "faithful subject" if Jefferson won the election, as seemed probable.

After Congress counted the electoral votes, Jefferson won the presidency by a majority of 73 to 65 for Adams. But did he? The original Constitution did not authorize separate candidacies for president and vice president. Each elector cast two votes with the top vote-getter, who secured a majority, becoming president and second-place finisher becoming vice president. In 1800, Jefferson's de-facto vice-presidential running mate, Aaron Burr of New York, tied Jefferson with seventy-three votes. Jefferson's supporters had failed in their plan to ensure that Burr received one less electoral vote.

The tie thrust the election into the lame duck U.S. House of Representatives with each of the sixteen states casting one vote. With no clear partisan majority in the House, Jeffersonians feared that the Federalists would stalemate the vote beyond the inauguration date of March 4 and install one of their own as president. The rumors of armed conflict spread across the land. Prominent pro-Jefferson Representative of Pennsylvania Albert Gallatin wrote, "Will the Federalists usurp the presidential powers? . . . would there be civil war." Some Jeffersonian state leaders threatened secession if the Federalists denied the will of voters. Adams accepted his fate as a defeated president. On January 20, 1801, he privately wrote, "I believe however upon the whole, I must be Farmer John of Stonyfield, and nothing more, (I hope nothing less) for the rest of my Life. The happiest Life it will be to me, (at least I think so) that I ever led." Two weeks later, as the House deliberations dragged on, he wrote despairingly, "Clouds black and gloomy hang over this country threatening a fierce tempest, arising merely from party conflicts. . . . I pray Heaven to dissipate the alarm."

Yet, the constitutional order prevailed without chaos or bloodshed. After thirty-six ballots, on February 17, 1801, with time to spare before Inauguration Day, a House majority elected Thomas Jefferson as the third president of the United States. Federalist James Bayard, Delaware's lone representative who controlled the state's vote, broke the deadlock by abandoning his support for Burr. Despite his disagreement with Jefferson on the issues, he feared that Burr threatened America's still fledgling democracy. Burr lacked "probity," Alexander Hamilton wrote to Bayard and was consumed with "an ambition which will be content with nothing less than permanent power in his own hands." He would cast aside the constitutional framework to establish a "system of the day, sufficient to serve his own turn, & not looking beyond himself."

Bayard responded that "the step was not taken until it was admitted on all hands that we must risk the Constitution and a civil war or take Mr. Jefferson." Although Adams declined to attend Jefferson's inauguration, twenty days later he wrote to the new president that "this part of the Union is in a state of perfect Tranquility and I see nothing to obscure your prospect of a quiet and prosperous Administration, which I heartily wish you."

Despite their hatred of Jefferson and "despite the rumors of civil war, despite the intense strain on the constitutional consensus, Federalists did not persist in prolonging the deadlock—as they might have— until after the expiration of Adams's term and then try to appoint one of their own allies," wrote Susan Dunn, a historian of the election. She noted that "although the potential for disruption had been real, no secession took place, no coup d'état, no attempts to change the Constitution, no military confrontations, no assassination." The Federalists, Dunn added, "were the first political incumbents in modern history" to peacefully cede power to their political opponents, however reluctantly.

The precedent set in 1800 lasted for close to 220 years, until 2020. In 1824, four major candidates ran for president after the first party system of Jeffersonians and Federalists had collapsed. War hero Andrew Jackson led with 41 percent of the electoral vote and Secretary of State John Quincy Adams followed with 31 percent. This lack of an electoral vote majority pitched the election into the House of Representatives for the second and last time in U.S. history. The Constitution did not obligate the House to choose the plurality winner. Instead, spurred on by Speaker Henry Clay, who despised Jackson, it chose Adams.

The defeated Jackson and the American people accepted this constitutionally sanctioned result. "Never was the usual courtesy of General Jackson more conspicuous," reported the *National Intelligencer*. "There was the laudable magnanimity in the manner in which he saluted Mr. Adams" as the election winner. "The Constitution has stood the test, without the occurrence of any of those dreadful events so dolefully predicted," wrote a commentator in the *Niles Weekly Register*. "The whole affair . . . is a magnificent commentary on our system of government and a glorious proof that 'errors of opinion may be safely tolerated, when reason is left free to combat them.'" When Adams appointed Clay as his secretary of state, then considered a stepping-stone to the presidency, Jackson charged the two men with a "corrupt bargain." However,

Jackson justly waited four years for revenge, defeating Adams in his bid for a second term.

In 1857, Congress debated the disposition of Wisconsin's five electoral votes, which a blizzard had delayed for delivery until a day after the legal deadline. When Congress convened in a joint session to count the electoral votes, the Senate's president pro-tempore, James Murray Mason, the grandson of Framer George Mason, presided. Vice President William King had died and there was at the time no procedure for replacing him. Mason ruled unilaterally that "nothing can be done here but to count the votes delivered to him by the tellers" who received the votes from the states. That "did not involve, in the opinion of the Chair, the validity or the invalidity of the vote of the State of Wisconsin."

Although the results in Wisconsin had no bearing on the outcome of an election that Democrat James Buchanan had won handily, Democratic Representative James Orr of South Carolina moved to reject the Wisconsin vote. Mason ruled him out of order. Several other legislators then challenged this unilateral decision. Senator John Crittenden of Kentucky, a member of the new Know-Nothing Party, asked whether "in assuming to declare the number of votes," the presiding officer was assuming "the privilege of determining a presidential election and saying who shall be President? I protest." Democratic Senator Andrew Butler of South Carolina said, "I will trust no man to determine for me who shall be President of the United States on his arbitrary decision." Democratic Senator Robert Toombs of Georgia asked, "suppose, as it might often happen, there was a double return from some State." Only the Senate and the House, not the presiding officer, he said, can "determine what are the votes. . . . It was a dangerous power to be entrusted to the Presiding Officer."

The Senate and the House debated the fate of Wisconsin's votes for two days. The lawmakers ultimately did not overrule Mason on the counting of Wisconsin's votes because an "Act of God" had prevented the electors from reaching the state capital on time. Congress left unresolved thorny issues on procedures for counting electoral votes when it mattered. Congress would not take up this issue until after the controverted election of 1876.

In 1876, during the final days of Reconstruction, Samuel J. Tilden, the governor of New York, won the popular vote against Republican Governor Rutherford B. Hayes of Ohio. The counting of electoral votes remained uncertain, pending the resolution of disputed votes in Florida, South Carolina, and Louisiana. Congress improvised by forming a special electoral commission controlled by the Republicans who voted along party lines to allot all the electoral votes in question to Hayes. He prevailed by one vote in the Electoral College.

Tilden and his supporters did not initiate legal proceedings to challenge the results. They made no call for violent resistance. There ensued "general rejoicing over the end of a contest which at one time promised to be so disastrous," reported the *New York Times*. The crowd that gathered at Hayes's inauguration represented "every State and almost every crossroad in the Union," with "not one man who is not ready to lift his hat to the new President, and to freely admit his title to the office upon which he is about to enter." On June 13, 1877, when Tilden finally conceded formally, he said, "If my voice could reach throughout our country and be heard in its remotest hamlet I would say, Be of good cheer. The Republic will live."

A decade later, Congress enacted the Electoral Count Act of 1887 ostensibly to clarify the resolution of election disputes. Republican Senator John Sherman of Ohio noted that "this bill affects a question that is more dangerous to the future of this country than probably any other." The procedure for counting electoral votes in Congress "is now without law or rule to govern the mode and manner of its procedure," he said. The act appeared to resolve certain questions. It seemingly barred the vice president from arbitrarily ruling on the validity of electoral votes from the states. Any objections must be submitted in writing by a member of each chamber, after which the House and the Senate would debate the matter separately. An objection could only be upheld by a majority vote of both houses.

But the law is prolix and convoluted, with gaping loopholes. It obliges states to establish procedures for the allocation of their electoral votes before an election. But it does not specify the role of courts in reviewing and modifying electoral procedures. The act also sets out an exception. It seems to authorize state legislatures to appoint electors following a "failed" election. Most authorities agree that this provision referred to an unforeseen, uncontrollable event such as a natural disaster—think of the Wisconsin blizzard of 1857. However, the meaning is undefined, and a partisan majority in a state legislature could attempt to unilaterally declare an election "failed" because of alleged electoral fraud. The act does not specify the role of the courts in resolving such a controversy. The law established a "safe harbor" day, which is six days before the Electoral College formally votes. Slates certified by this time are presumptively valid. But disputes over election results must presumably be settled prior to the safe harbor. Does that mean that a candidate or party can delay the "safe harbor," continuing to file lawsuits through the deadline? Do legal disputes include federal as well as state court challenges? Do they include appeals?

An attempted coup by a state legislature could result in multiple slates of electors submitted to Congress, with resolution unclear under the 1887 act. The law seems to suggest that the slate certified by the "executive" of the state would prevail in the absence of agreement by the House and the Senate. But some authorities dispute this interpretation. For example, what happens if the state supreme court declares invalid the slate certified by the governor or the slate is not certified prior to the "safe harbor" day? Would it require a vote of the two houses of Congress to resolve the dispute? What if a defeated president attempts to overturn the election results by declaring martial law and ordering a new election? The law does not specify if the electoral votes of a state are rejected, whether a majority is calculated for all electoral votes or votes minus the rejected count.

However, until 2020, no defeated candidate stooped to exploit these cracks in the law. In 1960, Republican Vice President Richard Nixon narrowly lost the presidency to challenger John F. Kennedy. Nixon resisted pressure by some within the GOP to lend his name or prestige to challenging the election. Nixon conceded defeat on election night. He declared in a gracious concession speech that "I have great faith that our people, Republicans, Democrats alike, will unite behind our next president."

In 2000, Democratic Vice President Al Gore quickly conceded after the U.S. Supreme Court halted the Florida recount with Bush ahead. "I accept the finality of this outcome," he said. "For the sake of our unity as a people and the strength of our democracy, I offer my concession." Four years later, some backers of losing Democrat John Kerry urged him to litigate alleged irregularities in the Ohio vote, which gave Bush his Electoral College majority. Kerry refused. He said that he had talked with President Bush "about the danger of division in our country and the need—the desperate need for unity, for finding the common ground, coming together." Kerry added that "in America, it is vital that every vote count, and that every vote be counted. But the outcome should be decided by voters, not a protracted legal process."

In 2005, two Democrats, Representative Stephanie Tubbs Jones of Ohio and Senator Barbara Boxer of California, objected in writing to the Ohio tally. This prompted separate votes in both chambers. Tubbs Jones said on the House floor that her objection "does not have at its root the hope or even the hint of overturning the victory of the president." Rather, the two lawmakers intended to call attention to the alleged voter suppression in Ohio. The Senate rejected the objection 74 to 1 and the House rejected it 267 to 31.

In 2020, however, Trump launched a concerted assault on results in swing states that he lost. This was a prearranged strategy unrelated to the merit of his disputes. On the Sunday before Election Day, Trump promised, "We're going to go in the night of, as soon as that election is over, we're going in with our lawyers." As anticipated, on election night, Trump claimed, "We already have won it," even as swing state officials were still counting millions of votes. Trump continued to claim that he won by a landslide if "legal, not illegal votes" were counted, even though Biden won the popular tally by some seven million votes and the electoral vote by 306 to 232.

Like a house built on straw, Trump's claims of fraud in the election blew apart under scrutiny. Dominion voting machines did not manufacture Biden votes or erase Trump's. A hand count of paper ballots by Republican officials in Georgia verified the machine count. The late Venezuelan autocrat Hugo Chavez did not rise from the grave to steal the election. Supposed dead voters turned out to be alive and well. A suitcase supposedly full of illegal ballots in Detroit was a box of camera material. Trump's votes were not rejected in Arizona because election officials forced voters into using Sharpie pens. Democrats had not programmed a supercomputer to erase Trump votes. A postal worker who claimed to have overheard election supervisors in Pennsylvania talking about illegally backdating late-arriving ballots recanted his story. Federal investigators debunked another bogus story by a trucker who claimed he had delivered many thousands of illegally filled-out ballots to Pennsylvania from a depot on Long Island.

Claims that states violated electoral laws by facilitating voting during the pandemic proved equally unfounded. That is why nearly ninety judges, including many appointed by Republican presidents and Trump himself, rejected some sixty-three lawsuits for a lack of factual or legal merit. With his election challenges toppling like dominoes, Trump backed what he called the "big one," a lawsuit that Texas Attorney General Ken Paxton filed on "safe harbor" day, December 8, 2020. Paxton petitioned the U.S. Supreme Court to overturn the election results of four other states that Biden won: Georgia, Michigan, Pennsylvania, and Wisconsin. A majority of Republicans in the U.S. House of Representatives signed on to the lawsuit, along with seventeen Republican state attorneys general.

Three days later, in an unsigned order, the Supreme Court rejected Paxton's petition. The three justices whom Trump had appointed to the high court did not dissent. Justice Samuel Alito, joined by Justice Clarence Thomas, said that the Court was constitutionally bound to hear a cross-state suit, but added that they would "not grant other relief." Even these most sympathetic justices would not credit Paxton's junk box full of false claims of fraud that the courts had already reviewed and rejected. Eventually, the U.S. Supreme Court, with the assent of Trump-appointed judges, rejected all Trump petitions to review lower court decisions. The Court put to rest claims already rejected by other courts on voter fraud and the allegation that several swing states had violated the U.S. Constitution's Electors Clause by using election rules that their state legislatures had not specifically authorized.

But Trump did not limit his quest to overturn the election to litigation only. He waged total war against the verdict of the voters by all conceivable means. He urged Republican members of election boards to decertify legitimate results. He became the first president to pressure state officials to declare a "failed election"—presumably based on his false claims of fraud—and discard the voters' will in favor of Trump electors. "It is difficult to imagine a worse, more undemocratic action by a sitting American president," said Republican Senator Mitt Romney of Utah. Yet, Trump had only just begun. In Georgia, the president asked Governor Brian Kemp, a conservative Republican and Trump supporter, to break state law and call a special legislative session to appoint Trump electors. When Kemp said he had no power to do so, Trump called on the governor to resign. "He is an obstructionist who refuses to admit that we won Georgia, BIG!" Trump tweeted. "Also won the other Swing States."

After the Electoral College voted on December 14, state officials in swing states continued to investigate fraud in the election. They came up empty. As of year-end 2020, Pennsylvania officials had charged just three voters with fraud, all Republicans. Wisconsin had charged one person and Michigan just two. Voters cast more than sixteen million ballots in these three states. The Texas Attorney General's Office spent twenty-two thousand hours looking for election fraud and closed only sixteen minor cases out of more than eleven million ballots cast in 2020.

By late December, even editors of conservative magnate Rupert Murdoch's fiercely pro-Trump *New York Post* had enough. "STOP THE INSANITY," read the paper's front page on December 28, 2020, in big, bright capital letters. "You lost the election," the *Post*'s editorial board wrote. "It's time to end this dark charade. You're cheering for an undemocratic coup. . . . If you insist on spending your final days in office threatening to burn it all down, that will be how you are remembered. Not as a revolutionary, but as the anarchist holding the match."

Trump disregarded that warning. He implored Vice President Pence to violate the Electoral Count Act on January 6, 2021, by unilaterally disqualifying Biden's electors and handing the election to Trump. This is what members of Congress feared during the 1857 debates over certifying Wisconsin's votes. Trump called on members of the House and Senate to challenge the results in key states. On January 2, Trump crossed the Rubicon into potential election tampering. He pressured Georgia's Republican Secretary of State Brad Raffensperger in an hour-long phone call to "find" just enough votes to reverse the election results. "I just want to find 11,780 votes, which is one more than we have because we won the state," Trump said. "We won it by hundreds of thousands of votes." Trump then issued a thinly veiled threat. After calling out Raffensperger for reporting what Trump falsely claimed were illegal results, the president said, "That's a criminal, that's a criminal offense. And you can't let that happen. That's a big risk to you and to Ryan, your lawyer."

Trump backed an eleventh-hour lawsuit brought by his ally, Republican Representative Louie Gohmert of Texas, that would authorize Pence to disallow the certified results in swing states and appoint Trump electors. A Trump-appointed federal district court judge rejected the lawsuit, and a panel of the Fifth Circuit Court of Appeals, consisting of two Reagan-appointed judges and one Trump-appointed judge, affirmed. In an unsigned order without dissent, the Supreme Court declined to take up the case. Still, Trump continued to pressure Vice President Pence and Republicans in Congress to reject certified votes and either appoint alternative slates of Trump electors or toss the election into the House of Representatives. Like Napoleon's legendary follower, Nicholas Chauvin, Pence had maintained unwavering devotion to Trump, but he finally balked at illegally attempting to decide an election unilaterally.

Trump plotted with Jeffrey Clark, whom Trump had installed as interim head of the civil division of the Department of Justice, for an extraordinary coup. Trump would oust Jeffrey Rosen, who became acting attorney general upon Barr's withdrawal, and replace him with Clark. The new top lawyer would have Justice officially back Trump's effort to overturn election results, despite its earlier finding of a clean election. The plot fizzled after senior Justice officials threatened to resign if the president replaced Rosen.

"Nothing remotely compares to this," said constitutional scholar Akhil Amar of Yale Law School. Trump's "actions since the election have threatened the very existence of our constitutional democracy. This looms large in the history of not just this administration, but the history of America. This is what history will remember most harshly."

After losing in court, Gohmert called for a violent response by Trump supporters. "You have no remedy," he said. "Basically, in effect, the ruling would be that you gotta go to the streets and be as violent as Antifa and BLM." Gohmert later tried to walk back this incitement to violence, but he could not unring that bell. Trump and his allies stoked the anger that Gohmert exploited. The president repeatedly called upon followers to "stop the steal" and fight to take back the country. On December 19, Trump tweeted, "Big protest in D.C. on January 6th. Be there, will be wild!" At a January 4 rally, he said of "liberal Democrats" that "they're not taking this White House—we're going to fight like hell." "All hell is going to break loose tomorrow," said soon-to-be-pardoned Steve Bannon on his January 5 podcast, entitled *War Room*. Trump's already pardoned Michael Flynn had told Trump's people that they were engaged "in a war against the forces of evil," and must "refuse to go to the funeral of our own independence."

John Dean, Richard Nixon's former White House counsel, said, "Incitement is not a single act; it is a process. It could be over several months." Olivia Troye, a former top aide to Pence, who left the White House in August 2020, warned on December 28, she was "very concerned that there will be violence on January 6th because the President himself is encouraging it. This is what he does. He tweets. He incites it." Trump's incitement hit a crescendo on January 6, when his loyalists stormed the U.S. Capitol. He lied again at an incendiary rally about a stolen election and said, "We're going to have to fight much harder. . . . We're going to walk down to the Capitol, and . . . you have to show strength, and you have to be strong." He called on the crowd to "demand that Congress do the right thing . . . fight like hell . . . you'll never take back our country with weakness."

During his more-than-an-hour-long harangue, Trump tossed in a few seemingly incongruous words. He said that the crowd should go to the closed Capitol and "peacefully and patriotically make your voices heard." It was a typical Trump escape hatch from inflammatory rhetoric, as, for example, when he charged that Mexico was sending America rapists and criminals, but added, "and some, I assume, are good people."

At the rally, the president's personal lawyer, Rudy Giuliani, called for "trial by combat." It is time to "start taking down names and kicking ass," said Republican Representative Mo Brooks of Alabama, a leader of the push to challenge the Electoral College results in Congress. "If you just roll over, if you don't fight in the face of glaring irregularities and statistical impossibilities . . . if you're going to be the zero and not the hero, we are coming for you," said Donald Trump Jr. The rally "should be a message to all the Republicans who have not been willing to actually fight." The rioters breached the defenses of an inadequate and unprepared Capitol Police, leaving in their wake several dead and many more injured.

Trump did not go on television to demand that his followers immediately stop the rampage and leave the Capitol. In real time, he watched their deadly riot unfold on television with some delight, eyewitnesses said. He did not summon a contingent of federally commanded armed National Guard forces assembled near the Capitol. He did not urgently call his secretaries of Defense or Homeland Security, or the director of the FBI.

On the contrary, Trump prevented the activation of the National Guard forces by demanding requests to move up the chain of command to the top. The National Guard Commander, General William

Walker, testified before a Senate committee on March 3, 2021. He said that "unusual" restrictions had been placed on the National Guard's deployment prior to January 6, contrary to the alert posture during the Black Lives Matter protests in June. The general said he had a contingent of about 150 guards ready to go to Capitol Hill within twenty minutes and that their help "could have made a difference." But Walker only got clearance from the Pentagon three hours and nineteen minutes after his request, much too late.

Trump failed to heed the pleas of Republicans in Congress, who, fearing for their lives, desperately tried calling him, with no response. "We are imploring the president to help, to stand up, to help defend the United States Capitol and the United States Congress, which was under attack," said Republican Representative Anthony Gonzalez of Ohio, no coward, but a former NFL tight end. "We are begging, essentially, and he was nowhere to be found." Republican House Leader Kevin McCarthy had reached Trump to ask for his help. Trump falsely tried to deflect blame for the mayhem on Antifa. When McCarthy responded that these were "Trump supporters," the president said, "Well, Kevin, I guess these people are more upset about the election than you are."

The most incriminating "smoking gun" tweet came just after 6 p.m. that day. It was so obviously compromising that Trump soon deleted it. He said, "These are the things and events that happen when a sacred landslide election victory is so unceremoniously & viciously stripped away from great patriots who have been badly & unfairly treated for so long. Go home with love & in peace. Remember this day forever!" In his own words, Trump admitted that the violent protest resulted from grievances over a supposedly stolen election. Yet, it was Trump himself who ginned up these grievances with a two-month drumbeat of lies that culminated in the fiery rhetoric of his January 6 rally. In simple terms, no incitement by Trump about the election, no insurrection. In his tweet, Trump passionately assured the rioters that they had acted like patriots. Their assault on the Capitol, he suggested, should be forever commemorated and cherished, not reviled.

Imagine if black Democrats had summoned a Black Lives Matter protest to the Capitol, saying it will be "wild," that you are "in a war against the forces of evil," and "have to fight like hell to get your country back." No doubt, Trump would have ringed the Capitol with thousands of heavily armed National Guard troops and federal agents. It would not have mattered if organizers had tossed in a line about protesting peacefully.

On January 13, 2021, the U.S. House voted to make Trump the first president in American history to suffer impeachment, not once, but twice. Liz Cheney, the third-ranking Republican in the U.S. House, voted for impeachment. "There has never been a greater betrayal by a president of the United States of his office and his oath to the Constitution," Cheney said. Ten Republicans voted for the only article on inciting insurgency, double the number of representatives who had previously voted to impeach a president of their party.

A month later, senators voted to convict Donald Trump by a fifty-seven to forty-three margin that fell short of the needed two-thirds vote. With seven Republicans joining all fifty Democrats, for the first time in history a bipartisan majority had voted to convict an impeached president. Many GOP senators who voted for acquittal did not exonerate the president but claimed that the Senate lacked jurisdiction over a former president, despite an earlier majority vote to the contrary.

The system for electing an American president survived in 2020 the onslaught by Trump and his enablers. But only barely. The outcome could have been more precarious if the election were any closer, and if Trump's party had held decisive control over both houses of Congress.

## THE FIX: REWRITE THE ELECTORAL COUNT ACT OF 1887 AND ADOPT OTHER ANTI-OBSTRUCTION MEASURES

The Electoral Count Act of 1887 must be updated and rewritten in clear and straightforward terms. A new law should make it clear that a "failed election" only means an election impeded by a natural disaster or similar calamity beyond the control of elected officials. It would prevent a candidate from delaying a count by launching last-minute suits and state legislatures from overriding their election results. To avoid throwing elections into the U.S. House, it should base electoral vote majorities on the number of electoral votes cast, if some are disqualified. The act should reaffirm the primacy of electors certified by a state government unless overturned by a timely decision of the state or U.S.

Supreme Court. The revised law would clearly reaffirm that the vice president only has a ministerial role in vote counting and lacks decision-making authority. It would set out the ground rules for filing a challenge in Congress to the previously certified electoral college votes and require challengers to explain their reasoning in writing. It would ban a president from using military or law enforcement personnel to interfere with an election or its results.

To prevent a sour grapes candidate from delaying and obstructing election results through repeated frivolous lawsuits, Congress should enact the Trial Abuse Reduction Act. It passed the U.S. House in 2017 but died in the Senate. The bill provides mandatory sanctions for filing a frivolous claim, putting some teeth into existing law. Remedies include "striking the pleadings, dismissing the suit, or other directives of a non-monetary nature, or, if warranted for effective deterrence, an order directing payment of a penalty into the court." The courts would still have the discretion to assess the claim as frivolous or not.

To protect civil rights litigation, the act clarifies that "nothing in this Act or an amendment made by this Act shall be construed to bar or impede the assertion or development of new claims, defenses, or remedies under Federal, State, or local laws, including civil rights laws, or under the Constitution of the United States." It does not change the strict standards for assessing whether a lawsuit is frivolous or not.

Congress needs to reform and increase funding for the nearly moribund Help America Vote Act of 2002. Enhanced funding combined with federal standards for election technology and administration would help states establish uniform best practices and upgrade their electoral systems. Federal standards should include a paper trail for all votes, an independent audit of voting machines, and standardized procedures for counting and recounting votes. The amended law should require as a condition of federal assistance that nonpartisan officials administer elections in the states.

## • *14* •

# Conclusion

### *Promoting Civic Virtue and Healing a Divided America*

> Where you see wrong or inequality or injustice, speak out, because this is your country. This is your democracy. Make it. Protect it. Pass it on.
>
> —U.S. Supreme Court Justice Thurgood Marshall, 1978

$\mathcal{P}$ropagandists in the Soviet Union celebrated their Constitution of 1936 as "the most democratic charter in the world." The Constitution ensured the right to free elections by universal suffrage. It upheld freedom of expression, press, and assembly. It established equality of status for all citizens and liberty of conscience, including religion. The Constitution guaranteed the right to work, to hold personal property, to enjoy rest and leisure, and to receive support in old age, sickness, or disability. It afforded protection from unreasonable arrests and interference with the confidentiality of correspondence. It proclaimed equal rights for women.

In a nation lacking traditions of democracy or human rights, these paper guarantees meant nothing. "The provisions of fundamental rights are included in the Constitution largely for propaganda reasons," wrote the American legal scholar Thomas E. Towe. The Soviet citizen, he said, "stands unprotected against the overwhelming power of the party leaders." The Soviet Constitution was "a veil of liberal phrases and premises over the guillotine in the background," concluded Isaac Deutscher, a Polish authority on Soviet history and a dedicated socialist.

Dictator Joseph Stalin, who ruled the Soviet Union from the mid-1920s until his death in 1953, ignored constitutional rights. He murdered his political opponents or imprisoned them in the Gulag Archipelago that stretched across remote regions of the land. Historians estimate that Stalin and his henchmen sent eighteen million persons to the Gulag system between 1930 and 1953, with some 1.5 million deaths.

Democracy briefly flared in post-Soviet Russia during the 1990s until extinguished by Russian President Vladimir Putin. Many of the democratic rights enshrined in the 1936 Constitution remain nominally in force. However, "Putin has worked to dismantle whatever inconvenient democratic institutions managed to take root," wrote Brian Grodsky, a political science professor at the University of Maryland, Baltimore County. "Free media outlets were shuttered. Civil society organizations were strangled. Electoral institutions were carefully manipulated to ensure Putin and the United Russia party backing him could not be beat."

This experience under the Soviet Constitution blares as a cautionary tale for democracy in the United States. Closing the loopholes of democracy after Trump is a necessary but insufficient condition for democracy to flourish again in the world's longest-running democratic republic. Both civic virtue and an enlivened system of checks and balances would safeguard democracy. James Madison, the nation's greatest exponent of balanced power, wrote about the progression of good people to good citizens and good government:

> But I go on this great republican principle, that the people will have virtue and intelligence to select men of virtue and wisdom. Is there no virtue among us? If there be not, we are in a wretched situation. No theoretical checks, no form of government, can render us secure. To suppose that any form of government will secure liberty or happiness without any virtue in the people, is a chimerical idea.

To nurture this elusive quality of civic virtue, the reforms proposed here represent a crucial step forward. Enforced laws cultivate virtue by changing hearts and minds. After enactment of the Civil Rights Act of 1964, most white southerners gradually came to reject the legal segregation of the races that had prevailed for nearly one hundred years. Before the 1967 Supreme Court ruling overturning laws against interracial marriage, the National Opinion Research Center (NORC) found a substantial majority in favor of such laws. Just five years later, support had plummeted to only 38 percent.

Much work remains to counter the corrosive effects of Donald Trump's sowing of divisions among Americans. President George Washington so feared the dangers of a divided nation that he opposed the formation of political parties and advocated governing by consensus. Factionalism, Washington said, "agitates the community with ill-founded jealousies and . . . foments occasionally riot and insurrection."

Trump took presidential leadership to the opposite extreme of Washington's vision. In Trump's America, the opposition becomes disloyal—not just wrong on the issues, but immoral and un-American. Larry Diamond, an expert on democratic governance at the conservative Hoover Institution, said Trump "has massive responsibility for creating the normative atmosphere in which extremism, hatred, racial bigotry, and violent imagery have prospered and metastasized."

Social psychologist Richard Koenigsberg notes that Trump fits within a historical pattern of marginalizing the so-called dangerous other. He "builds upon one of the central templates" of modern Western history, the radical nationalism that scapegoats with lies a "dangerous other." The scapegoat could be called "a Jew or a Bolshevik or a homosexual" or "a Mexican, a Muslim, a Syrian, an Arab or an immigrant." It "doesn't matter" the name. "At the heart of radical nationalism is the idea or belief that *certain groups of people are the source of the nation's problems—and suffering.*" The nation can return to greatness only "if certain classes of people" are either "denied entry" or "removed."

The fomenting of "us and them" divisions among Americans transcends Trump and his enablers. A March 2021 article by Glenn Ellmers in *American Mind*, published by the Claremont Institute, a respected conservative think tank, claimed that "most people living in the United States today—certainly more than half—are not Americans in any meaningful sense of the term." Like white insurrectionists throughout American history, he marginalizes and dehumanizes Americans who are different from himself. "It is not obvious what we should call these citizen-aliens, these non-American Americans; but they are something else," he wrote. Ellmers suggests a violent response to the threatened collapse of real America. "The U.S. Constitution no longer works," he said. Instead, "accept the fact that what we need is a counter-revolution.

Learn some useful skills, stay healthy, and get strong. (One of my favorite weightlifting coaches likes to say, 'Strong people are harder to kill, and more useful generally.')" In an earlier January 2020 essay, Ellmers wrote, "not for the first time in our nation's history, if this state of affairs continues, force may be embraced as the only alternative when reason fails."

Ellmers is no outlier. Per a January 2021 American Perspectives survey, 39 percent of Republicans agreed that "if elected leaders won't protect America, the people must act—even if that means violence." A February 2021 CBS News poll found that 57 percent of Republicans considered Democrats as "enemies" rather than as the "political opposition."

Yet, there is a danger that there is no legal fix, no "ombudsman of division" who can prevent a future president and others from fomenting the same level of division. But there are reforms that can go a long way toward healing a divided nation and nurturing civil virtue.

Academic research shows that education predicts political and civic participation, tolerance, confidence in public institutions, critical thinking, and political knowledge. According to University of North Carolina, Chapel Hill sociology professor Andrew J. Perrin, the independent effect of education holds "particularly for students with relatively low prior propensity to attend college."

High costs and a lack of information prevent too many young Americans from attending college. The targeted, outreach campaign for low-income students at the University of Michigan provides a model for the nation. The program encourages well-qualified, less affluent students to apply to the university, with study free of tuition and fees. The University sends personalized mailers to prospective students rather than waiting for them to apply and fill out complex financial assistance forms. A study published by the National Bureau of Economic Research found that the program works so well that 28 percent of students receiving the mailer enrolled in the university, compared to just 13 percent in a control group. The study found that approximately a quarter of the group enrolled in the program would not otherwise have attended any college.

The Michigan model should guide policy in each American state, with financial support from the federal government. These investments will pay off in less welfare and crime, and increased productivity from a better-educated people. The model works not only for flagship institutions like the University of Michigan, but also for every college and university within a state system. Texas, for example, has adopted a "10 percent plan" that guarantees admission and free tuition for a state college or university to all students in the top 10 percent of their high school class.

Before college, elementary and secondary school students could benefit from revised and refreshed education in history and civics. The Trump administration proposed an official guide to the teaching of history in a *1776 Report*, which ignores historical studies to follow Trump's political biases. The report states that American slavery was justified as a standard practice for the times. It says that America led the world in ending slavery, even though it did so only after a civil war in 1865, compared to Mexico in 1829, Britain in 1833, and France and Denmark in 1848.

The report cites progressivism as an enemy of America on a par with communism and fascism. It transmutes Martin Luther King Jr. into a radical libertarian, even though he pushed beyond "colorblindness" to back unions, affirmative action, federal employment programs, and other measures against structural racism and economic inequality. Native Americans and immigrants find no place in its story. Neither does the labor of slaves that helped build the nation and sustained its economy for centuries. Women gain only glancing notice.

We can do much better. Now that President Biden has properly buried the biased *1776 Report*, he should appoint a new historical commission of leading historians who would draw on the best scholarship. It would not counter the Trump report with a liberal version of American history. A revised guideline would explore the history of the world's most robust and diverse society in all its nuances and complexities. It would highlight differing interpretations of the American past and include the so-called forgotten peoples, who are often neglected in historical texts. It would tell the story of slaves and Native Americans, women, and immigrants. But it would explore the often overlooked history of America's vibrant conservative movement, as, for example, in my own book, *White Protestant Nation: The Rise of the American Conservative Movement*.

This would be an evolving, interactive project, not a document carved in stone like the *1776 Report*. It would be subject to addition and revision, reflecting a diversity of views and sensitivity to new methods, evidence, and ideas. "Disagreement is a feature, not a bug, of our constitutional democracy; the question is whether we can learn to disagree productively," wrote professors Danielle Allen of Harvard and Paul Carrese of Arizona State universities. They are members of the executive committee of the Educating for American Democracy Project. Their report provides "a strategy for ensuring that all the nation's learners come to understand, appreciate—and productively use and debate—our form of government and civic life." The strategy would counter the efforts by Republicans in the states to chill the teaching of race through the pretext of banning "critical race theory."

Local governments and school boards are primarily responsible for education. No plan of education can succeed without the commitment of teachers, students, parents, and community leaders. However, the *Educating for American Democracy Report* suggests how the federal government can help schools incorporate an inclusive but a nuanced vision of U.S. history and civics into their teaching and curricula. The federal government has the resources to build a robust database of primary sources for American history for use in schools. It can support innovation in educational funding, and finance demonstration projects in local communities. It can foster through workshops and seminars, grassroots debate, discussion, and input the evolving project of understanding America's past. The Department of Education can shift priorities to emphasize support for history and civics as well as technical disciplines. "Science and technology revolutionize our lives," wrote the historian Arthur M. Schlesinger Jr., "but memory, tradition, and myth frame our response."

To bond young people together and put them in contact with persons different from themselves in race, religion, class, culture, and political beliefs, Congress should mandate a year of national service. Such service to country brings people out of isolation and into a diverse community that closes, not widens, divides. "When service is seen as a bridge to genuine political and civic responsibility, it can strengthen democratic government and foster the republican virtues," wrote journalist E.J. Dionne Jr. and Kayla Meltzer Drogosz, the senior research analyst for the project on religion and civil society at the Brookings Institution.

We should break the grip of wealthy special interests on American politics and promote civic participation by ordinary citizens. To sweep away the politics of dark money, Congress should require all groups engaged in electoral politics to disclose donations and expenses to the Federal Election Commission. It should ban the use of shell companies as intermediaries for secret payments and impose strict disclosure requirements on lobbyists and their clients. As proposed by Lee Drutman of the New America Foundation, Congress can break the lobbying monopoly on access to information. It should improve the government's website that lists the bills that come before Congress with a free and open forum for citizen debate. Congress should put in place a voluntary system for publicly funding federal political campaigns and encourage states to do the same. As proposed by the Brennan Center for Social Justice, a model program would complement, rather than supersede, private fund-raising.

President Joe Biden designated his Inauguration Day, January 20, 2021, as an official "National Day of Unity." But that gesture does not suffice. By executive order, the president should proclaim a National Unity Week on certain dates each year. American leaders should encourage schools, colleges, and civic organizations to discuss democratic values and hold contests on the best ideas to prevent bullying, stereotypes, hateful speeches, and violence. Models exist for a national initiative. The National Bullying Prevention Center in Minneapolis, Minnesota, sponsors each year a voluntary Unity Day. The nonprofit group Braver Angels organizes "Race Conversations" at the local level to "talk about race in an inquisitive, non-judgmental way." Its "Red-Blue" workshops bring together "evenly divided groups of conservatives and liberals, or 'reds' and 'blues,' for a series of exercises designed to help participants clarify disagreements, reduce stereotyped thinking, and discover common values."

The safeguard of democracy is more democracy. Americans should celebrate the election of 2020. Voters turned out in record numbers for an election that President Trump's cybersecurity head Christopher Krebs called the "most secure in U.S. history." This is how democracy should work, with buoyant participation and fair voting. Voters rewarded both parties in 2020. Democrats won the presidency and control of the U.S. Senate (barely). Republicans picked up U.S. House and state legislative seats.

In the long run, the 2020 election may either divide or unite Americans. Fueled by Donald Trump's lies about a stolen election, an

AP-NORC poll in early February 2021 revealed that some two-thirds of Republicans denied that voters legitimately elected Biden as president. Democrats in the poll affirmed Biden's legitimacy. With positions on voting rights falling along party lines, the nation is crashing toward two separate democracies. We risk putting in one set of rules for Republican-dominated states and another for majority Democratic states. The right to vote for Americans may become dependent on where they live, just as it once depended on their property, race, or gender.

Dual systems of voting divided America from the late nineteenth century through the enactment of the Voting Rights Act of 1965. During this near century of history, voting rights for African Americans turned upon whether they lived in northern states or in the Jim Crow South. To keep voting rights from breaking along state lines and sustain dynamic turnout, we need the reforms detailed in chapter 11. To uphold majority rule, America needs to reform the Senate, with the collateral benefit of rebalancing the Electoral College.

Congress enacted the Voting Rights Act only after activists risked their lives on "Bloody Sunday," March 7, 1965. As they marched for the vote across the Edmund Pettus Bridge in Selma, Alabama, state troopers attacked them with nightsticks, tear gas, and police dogs. As in the civil rights era, new voting reforms are possible today only if the people demand it. "Voting is the foundation stone of political action," said Martin Luther King Jr. A secure vote empowers Americans to become participants in government and opens the door to other democratic reforms.

# Select Bibliography

## INTRODUCTION

Applebaum, Anne. (2020). *Twilight of Democracy: The Seductive Lure of Authoritarianism*. Doubleday.

Banner, James M., Jr. (2019). *Presidential Misconduct: From George Washington to Today*. New Press.

Freedom House. (4 March 2020). *NEW REPORT: Freedom in the World 2020 Finds Established Democracies Are in Decline*. https://freedomhouse.org/article/new-report-freedom-world-2020-finds-established-democracies-are-decline.

Gessen, Masha. (2020). *Surviving Autocracy*. Riverhead.

Hennessey, Susan, and Benjamin Wittes. (2020). *Unmaking the Presidency: Donald Trump's War on the World's Most Powerful Office*. Farrar, Straus and Giroux.

Lepore, Jill. (2019). *These Truths: A History of the United States*. W. W. Norton.

Levitsky, Steven, and Daniel Ziblatt. (2018). *How Democracies Die*. Crown.

Roser, Max. (June 2019). *Democracy*. Our World in Data. https://ourworldindata.org/democracy.

Rucker, Philip, and Carol Leonnig. (2020). *A Very Stable Genius: Donald J. Trump's Testing of America*. Penguin.

## CHAPTER 1: DOING WHATEVER I WANT: CONTROLLING AUTOCRACY

Burke, John P. (2016). *Presidential Power: Theories and Dilemmas*. Routledge.

Cooper, Philip J. (2014). *By Order of the President: The Use & Abuse of Executive Direct Action*. 2nd ed. University Press of Kansas.

Federal Register. (n.d.). *Executive Orders.* https://www.federalregister.gov/presidential-documents/executive-orders.

Howell, William G. (2003). *Power Without Persuasion: The Politics of Direct Presidential Action.* Princeton University Press.

Kitrosser, Heidi. (2015). *Reclaiming Accountability: Transparency, Executive Power, and the U.S. Constitution.* University of Chicago Press.

Marcus, Maeva. (1994). *Truman and the Steel Seizure Case: The Limits of Presidential Power.* Duke University Press.

Peters, Gerhard, and John T. Woolley. (2021). *Executive Orders.* The American Presidency Project. https://www.presidency.ucsb.edu/node/323876.

Rozell, Mark J., and Mitchel A. Sollenberger. (2020). *Executive Privilege: Presidential Power, Secrecy, and Accountability.* University Press of Kansas.

Thompson, Frank J., et al. (2020). *Trump, the Administrative Presidency, and Federalism.* Brookings Institution.

Waslin, Michele. (2020). The Use of Executive Orders and Proclamations to Create Immigration Policy: Trump in Historical Perspective. *Journal on Migration and Human Security*, 8.

## CHAPTER 2: CONGRESS BE DAMNED: RESTORING ACCOUNTABILITY

Baker, Jean H. (2004). *James Buchanan.* St. Martin's.

Cole, Lance, and Stanley M. Brand. (2010). *Congressional Investigations and Oversight: Case Studies and Analysis.* Carolina Academic.

Denault, Robert J. (2021). Not a King: President Trump and the Case for Presidential Subpoena Reform. *Duke Journal of Constitutional Law & Public Policy Sidebar*, 16.

Fisher, Louis. (2014). *Constitutional Conflicts Between Congress and the President.* 6th ed. University Press of Kansas.

Garvey, Todd. (27 March 2019). *Congressional Subpoenas: Enforcing Executive Branch Compliance.* Congressional Research Service. https://fas.org/sgp/crs/misc/R45653.pdf.

Hempowicz, Liz. (25 March 2021). *POGO Calls on Congress to Improve Its Capacity for Oversight.* https://www.pogo.org/testimony/2021/03/pogo-calls-on-congress-to-improve-its-capacity-for-oversight/.

Kriner, Douglas L., and Eric Schickler. (2016). *Investigating the President: Congressional Checks on Presidential Power.* Princeton University Press.

LaPira, Thomas M., Lee Drutman, and Kevin R. Kosar, eds. (2020). *Congress Overwhelmed: The Decline in Congressional Capacity and Prospects for Reform.* University of Chicago Press.

Reynolds, Molly E. (4 December 2019). *Improving Congressional Capacity to Address Problems and Oversee the Executive Branch.* Brookings Institution. https://www.brookings.edu/policy2020/bigideas/improving-congressional -capacity-to-address-problems-and-oversee-the-executive-branch/.

United States House of Representatives, Permanent Select Committee on Intelligence. (December 2019). *The Trump-Ukraine Impeachment Inquiry Report.* https://intelligence.house.gov/uploadedfiles/the_trump-ukraine_im peachment_inquiry_report.pdf.

## CHAPTER 3: RUSSIA IS LISTENING: DEFENDING AMERICA'S SOVEREIGNTY

Bolton, John. (2020). *The Room Where It Happened: A White House Memoir.* Simon & Schuster.

Gaughan, Anthony J. (2019). Putin's Revenge: The Foreign Threat to American Campaign Finance Law. *Howard Law Journal,* 62.

Mueller III, Robert S. (2019). *The Mueller Report.* Melville House.

National Intelligence Council. (10 March 2021). *Foreign Threats to the 2020 US Federal Elections.* https://www.dni.gov/files/ODNI/documents/assessments/ ICA-declass-16MAR21.pdf.

Office of the Director of National Intelligence. (9 April 2021). *Annual Threat Assessment of the US Intelligence Community.* https://www.dni.gov/files/ ODNI/documents/assessments/ATA-2021-Unclassified-Report.pdf.

Rid, Thomas. (2020). *Active Measures: The Secret History of Disinformation and Political Warfare.* Farrar, Straus, and Giroux.

Unger, Craig. (2021). *American Kompromat: How the KGB Cultivated Donald Trump, and Related Tales of Sex, Greed, Power, and Treachery.* Dutton.

United States Department of the Treasury. (15 April 2021). *Treasury Escalates Sanctions Against Russian Government's Attempts to Influence US Elections.* https://home.treasury.gov/news/press-releases/jy0126.

United States Senate, Select Committee on Intelligence. (18 August 2020). *Report on Russian Active Measures Campaigns and Interference in the 2016 U.S. Election, Volume 5: Counterintelligence Threats and Vulnerabilities.* https:// www.intelligence.senate.gov/sites/default/files/documents/report_volume5 .pdf.

Weiner, Tim. (2020). *The Folly and the Glory: America, Russia, and Political Warfare, 1945–2020.* Henry Holt.

Weissmann, Andrew. (2020). *Where Law Ends: Inside the Mueller Investigation.* Random House.

Zaulauf, Barry A. IC Analytic Ombudsman, Office of the Director of National Intelligence. (6 January 2021). *Independent IC Analytic Ombudsman's Report on Politicization of Intelligence.* https://fas.org/irp/eprint/politicization.pdf.

## CHAPTER 4: A PRESIDENCY
## BUILT ON LIES: RECLAIMING TRUTH

Alterman, Eric. (2020). *Lying in State: Why Presidents Lie—And Why Trump Is Worse.* Basic.

Carpenter, Amanda. (2018). *Gaslighting America: Why We Love It When Trump Lies to Us.* Broadside.

Donovan, Joan. (12 October 2020). Trolling for Truth on Social Media. *Scientific American.* https://www.scientificamerican.com/article/trolling-for-truth-on-social-media/.

Katz, James E., and Kate K. Mays, eds. (2019). *Journalism and Truth in an Age of Social Media.* Oxford University Press.

Koenigsberg, Richard A. (2011). *The Psychoanalysis of Racism, Revolution, and Nationalism.* Library of Social Science.

O'Neill, Cathy. (2017). *Weapons of Math Destruction: How Big Data Increases Inequality and Threatens Democracy.* Crown.

Orlowski, Jeff. (Director). (2020). *The Social Dilemma: A Netflix Original* [Film]. Netflix. https://www.netflix.com/title/81254224.

Persily, Nathaniel. (2020). *Social Media and Democracy.* Cambridge University Press.

Reedy, George E. (1970). *The Twilight of the Presidency.* World Publishing.

Sinha, G. Alex. (2020). Lies, Gaslighting and Propaganda. *Buffalo Law Review*, 68.

Smith, David Norman. (2019). Authoritarianism Reimagined: The Riddle of Trump's Base. *Sociological Quarterly*, 60.

*Washington Post* Fact Checker Staff. (2020). *Donald Trump and His Assault on Truth: The President's Falsehoods, Misleading Claims and Flat-Out Lies.* Scribner.

Woodward, Bob. (2020). *Rage.* Simon & Schuster.

Zuboff, Shoshana. (2020). *The Age of Surveillance Capitalism: The Fight for a Human Future at the New Frontier of Power.* PublicAffairs.

## CHAPTER 5: CORRUPT JUSTICE: REDEEMING LAW ENFORCEMENT

Center for Ethics and the Rule of Law Ad Hoc Working Group in Partnership with Citizens for Responsibility and Ethics in Washington. (12 October 2020). *Report on the Department of Justice and the Rule of Law under the Tenure of Attorney General William Barr.* Center for Ethics and the Rule of Law: University of Pennsylvania. https://www.law.upenn.edu/live/files/10900 -report-on-the-doj-and-the-rule-of-law.

Cho, Rebecca, Louis Cholden-Brown, and Marcello Figueroa. (2020). *Toward an Independent Administration of Justice: Proposals to Insulate the Department of Justice from Improper Political Interference.* Fordham Law Archive of Scholarship and History. https://ir.lawnet.fordham.edu/faculty_scholarship/1102.

Coan, Andrew. (2019). *Prosecuting the President: How Special Prosecutors Hold Presidents Accountable and Protect the Rule of Law.* Oxford University Press.

Cossin, Joshua. (25 June 2020). DOJ Officials Deliver Congressional Testimony on Politicization under Barr. *Jurist: Legal News and Commentary.* https://www.jurist.org/news/2020/06/doj-officials-deliver-congressional -testimony-on-politicization-under-barr/.

Crouch, Jeffrey. (2008). The Law: Presidential Misuse of the Pardon Power. *Presidential Studies Quarterly*, 38.

Foster, Michael A. (14 January 2020). Presidential Pardons: Overview and Selected Legal Issues. *Congressional Research Service.* https://crsreports.congress.gov/product/pdf/R/R46179.

Reynolds, Glenn H. (2018). Congressional Control of Presidential Pardons. *Nevada Law Journal Forum*, 2.

Stewart, James E. (2019). *Deep State: Trump, the FBI, and the Rule of Law.* Penguin.

United States House of Representatives, Committee on the Judiciary. (31 December 2020). *No President Is Above the Law Act of 2020.* https://www.govinfo.gov/content/pkg/CRPT-116hrpt705/html/CRPT-116hrpt705.htm.

United States House of Representatives, Government Reform Committee. (14 May 2002). *Justice Undone: Clemency Decisions in the Clinton White House, Together with Minority Views.* https://www.congress.gov/congressional -report/107th-congress/house-report/454/1.

Wehle, Kimberly L. (2021). Law and the OLC's Article II Immunity Memos. *Stanford Law & Policy Review.* 32.

## CHAPTER 6: ENEMIES OF THE
## PEOPLE: PROTECTING A FREE PRESS

Boczkowski, Pablo J., and Zizi Papacharissi, eds. (2018). *Trump and the Media.* MIT Press.

Carlson, Matt, Sue Robinson, and Seth C. Lewis. (2020). Digital Press Criticism: The Symbolic Dimensions of Donald Trump's Assault on U.S. Journalists as the "Enemy of the People." *Digital Journalism.* https://www.tandfonline.com/doi/abs/10.1080/21670811.2020.1836981?journalCode=rdij20.

Downie Jr., Leonard. (April 2020). *The Trump Administration and the Media: Attacks on Press Credibility Endanger US Democracy and Global Press Freedom.* Committee to Protect Journalists. https://cpj.org/wp-content/uploads/2020/04/cpj_usa_2020.pdf.

Frantzich, Stephen E. (2018). *Presidents and the Media: The Communicator in Chief.* Routledge.

Gunther, Richard, Paul A. Beck, and Erik C. Nisbet. (February 2018). Fake News Did Have a Significant Impact on the Vote in the 2016 Election: Original Full-Length Version with Methodological Appendix. *The Conversation.* https://cpb-us-w2.wpmucdn.com/u.osu.edu/dist/d/12059/files/2015/03/Fake-News-Piece-for-The-Conversation-with-methodological-appendix-11d0ni9.pdf.

Holan, Angie Drobnic. (2017). The Media's Definition of Fake News vs. Donald Trump's. *First Amendment Law Review*, 16.

Holzer, Harold. (2020). *The Presidents vs. the Press: The Endless Battle Between the White House and the Media—From the Founding Fathers to Fake News.* Dutton.

Natividad, Ivan. (27 January 2021). How Did Trump Change American Journalism? *Berkeley News.* https://news.berkeley.edu/2021/01/27/how-did-trump-change-american-journalism/.

Stelter, Brian. (2020). *Hoax: Donald Trump, Fox News, and the Dangerous Distortion of Truth.* Atria.

Tamul, Daniel, et al. (2020). All the President's Tweets: Effects of Exposure to Trump's "Fake News" Accusations on Perceptions of Journalists, News Stories, and Issue Evaluation. *Mass Communication and Society*, 23.

Vosoughi, Soroush, Deb Roy, and Sinan Aral. (2018). The Spread of True and False News Online. *Science*, 359.

## CHAPTER 7: PROFITS ABOVE PATRIOTISM: POLICING CONFLICTS OF INTEREST

Block, Samantha. (2018). It Is All About the Money: Presidential Conflicts of Interest. *Harvard Law School Journal of Legislation*, 58.

Chayes, Sarah. (2020). *On Corruption in America and What Is at Stake*. Knopf.

Citizens for Responsibility and Ethics in Washington (CREW). (24 September 2020). *President Donald Trump's 3,400 Conflicts of Interest*. https://www.citizensforethics.org/reports-investigations/crew-reports/president-trumps-3400-conflicts-of-interest/.

Gerson, Pedro. (2020). Return of the King: Corruption Backsliding in America. *Cardozo Journal of International, Comparative, Policy & Ethics Law Review*, 3.

Kibler, Marissa L. (2019). The Foreign Emoluments Clause: Tracing the Framers' Fears about Foreign Influence over the President. *New York University Annual Survey of American Law*, 74.

Sills, Deborah Samuel. (2018). The Foreign Emoluments Clause: Protecting Our National Security Interests. *Journal of Law and Policy*, 26.

Torres-Spelliscy, Ciara. (2019). From a Mint on a Hotel Pillow to an Emolument. *Mercer Law Review*, 70.

Teachout, Zephyr. (2014). *Corruption in America*. Harvard University Press.

## CHAPTER 8: POLITICAL CLEANSING: STOPPING FAVORITISM, CRONYISM, AND NEPOTISM

Brannon, Valerie C. (28 May 2021). *The Vacancies Act: A Legal Overview*. Congressional Research Service. https://fas.org/sgp/crs/misc/R44997.pdf.

Effective Government for the American People. (11 June 2017). What Is the Vacancies Act? *Partnership for Public Service*. https://presidentialtransition.org/wp-content/uploads/sites/6/2017/11/Partnership_Vacancies_Act_FAQ.pdf.

Emerson, Blake, and Jon D. Michaels (2021). Abandoning Presidential Administration: A Civic Governance Agenda to Promote Democratic Equality and Guard against Creeping Authoritarianism. *UCLA Law Review Discourse*, 68.

Gilens, Martin, and Benjamin Page. (2014). Testing Theories of American Politics: Elites, Interest Groups, and Average Citizens. *Perspectives on Politics*, 12.

Glicksman, Robert L., and Richard E. Levy. (2020). Restoring ALJ Independence. *Minnesota Law Review*, 105.

Government Accountability Project Press Release. (10 March 2021). Department of Justice Whistleblowers File Complaints Accusing Outgoing Trump Administration Official of Politicizing the Career Civil Service Promotion Process. *Government Accountability Project*. https://whistleblower.org/department-of-justice/press-release-department-of-justice-whistleblowers-file-complaints-accusing-outgoing-trump-administration-official-of-politicizing-the-career-civil-service-promotion-process/.

Kellough, J. Edward, Lloyd G. Nigro, and Gene A. Brewer. (2010). Civil Service Reform under George W. Bush: Ideology, Politics, and Public Personnel Administration. *Review of Public Personnel Administration*, 30.

Lewis, David E. (2008). *The Politics of Presidential Appointments: Political Control and Bureaucratic Performance*. Princeton University Press.

Vladeck, Steven. (Fall 2020). Good Government Paper No. 7: Executive Branch Vacancies. *Just Security*. https://www.justsecurity.org/72980/good-governance-paper-no-7-executive-branch-vacancies/.

## CHAPTER 9: GOVERNING IN
## THE DARK: EXPANDING TRANSPARENCY

Bumgarner, John R. (1994). *The Health of the Presidents: The 41 United States Presidents through 1993 from a Physician's Point of View*. McFarland.

Dharia, Megha, et al. (2020). Proposals for Improving Transparency in Presidential Campaigns. *Democracy and the Constitution Clinic, Fordham University School of Law*. https://www.fordham.edu/download/downloads/id/14399/What_Should_Presidential_Candidates_Tell_Us_About_Themselves_Democracy_Clinic.pdf.

Dudding, Sasha. (2021) Spinning Secrets: The Dangers of Selective Declassification. *Yale Law Journal*, 130.

Fenster, Mark. (2021). Populism and Transparency: The Political Core of an Administrative Norm. *University of Cincinnati Law Review*, 89.

Government Accountability Project. (22 February 2021). *Request for Swift Presidential Leadership to Make Transparency a Top Priority for the Biden Administration*. https://whistleblower.org/letter/request-for-swift-presidential-leadership-to-make-transparency-a-top-priority-for-the-biden-administration/.

Mistry, Kaeten, and Hannah Gurman, eds. (2020). *Whistleblowing Nation: The History of National Security Disclosures and the Cult of State Secrecy*. Columbia University Press.

National Security Archive. (22 April 2019). *35+ Years of Freedom of Information Action.* https://nsarchive.gwu.edu/briefing-book/foia/2019-04-18/redactions-declassified-file.

Pallitto, Robert M., and William G. Weaver. (2007). *Presidential Secrecy and the Law.* Johns Hopkins University Press.

Petriello, David. (2016). *A Pestilence on Pennsylvania Avenue: The Impact of Disease upon the American Presidency.* American History.

Relyea, Harold C. (11 February 2008). Security Classified and Controlled Information: History, Status, and Emerging Management Issues. *Congressional Research Service.* https://fas.org/sgp/crs/secrecy/RL33494.pdf.

United States House of Representatives, Committee on Oversight and Government Reform. (7 December 2006). *Hearing, Examining the Costs of Overclassification on Transparency and Security.* https://fas.org/spg/congress/2016/overclass.pdf.

Wagner, A. Jay. (2021). Pandering, Priority or Political Weapon: Presidencies, Political Parties & The Freedom of Information Act. *Communication Law and Policy*, 26.

Webb, Romany, Lauren Kurtz, and Susan Rosenthal. (2020). When Politics Trump Science: The Erosion of Science-Based Regulation. *Environmental Law Reporter*, 50.

## CHAPTER 10: A MILITARIZED NATION: SEPARATING THE MILITARY FROM POLITICS

Andreas, Peter. (2020). *Killer High: A History of War in Six Drugs.* Oxford University Press.

Elsea, Jennifer K. (4 January 2021). Defense Primer: Legal Authorities for the Use of Military Forces. *Congressional Research Service.* crsreports/congress.gov/product/pdf/IF/IF10539.

Golby, Jim. (18 June 2020). America's Politicized Military Is a Recipe for Disaster. *Foreign Policy.* https://foreignpolicy.com/2020/06/18/us-military-politics-trump-election-campaign/.

Harvard Law Review Association. (1968). Riot Control and the Use of Federal Troops. *Harvard Law Review*, 81.

Herspring, Dale R. (2005). *The Pentagon and the Presidency: Civil-Military Relations from FDR to George W. Bush.* University of Kansas Press.

Karlin, Mara, and Jim Golby. (12 June 2020). *The Case for Rethinking the Politicization of the Military.* Brookings Institution. https://www.brookings.edu/blog/order-from-chaos/2020/06/12/the-case-for-rethinking-the-politicization-of-the-military/.

Larson, Eric V., and John E. Peters. (2001). Overview of the Posse Comitatus Act. *Rand Corporation*. https://www.rand.org/content/dam/rand/pubs/monograph_reports/MR1251/MR1251.AppD.pdf.

Scheips, Paul J. (2002). The Role of Federal Military Forces in Domestic Disorders, 1945–1992. *Center of Military History, United States Army*. https://fas.org/man/eprint/disorders.pdf.

## CHAPTER 11: VOTER SUPPRESSION: RESTORING THE FRANCHISE

Anderson Carol. (2018). *One Person, No Vote: How Voter Suppression Is Destroying Our Democracy*. Bloomsbury.

Bell, Richard C. (2020). *Voting: The Ultimate Act of Resistance: The Real Truth from the Voting Rights Battlefields*. Word Association.

Brennan Center for Justice. (1 April 2021). *Voting Laws Roundup*. https://www.brennancenter.org/our-work/research-reports/voting-laws-roundup-march-2021.

Cottrell, David, Michael C. Herron, and Sean J. Westwood. (2018). An Exploration of Donald Trump's Allegations of Massive Voter Fraud in the 2016 General Election. *Electoral Studies*, 51.

Grimmer, Justin. (3 February 2021). No Evidence for Voter Fraud: A Guide to Statistical Claims about the 2020 Election. *Hoover Institution*. https://www.hoover.org/research/no-evidence-voter-fraud-guide-statistical-claims-about-2020-election.

Jentleson, Adam. (2021). *Kill Switch: The Rise of the Modern Senate and the Crippling of American Democracy*. Liveright.

Keyssar, Alexander. (2009). *The Right to Vote: The Contested History of Democracy in the United States*. Basic.

Kousser, J. Morgan. (2015). So the Facts of Voting Rights Support Chief Justice Robert's Opinion in Shelby County? *Transatlantica*, 1.

Lichtman, Allan J. (2018). *The Embattled Vote in America: From the Founding to the Present*. Harvard University Press.

Pennycook, Gordon, and David D. Rand. (11 January 2021). Examining False Beliefs about Voter Fraud in the Wake of the 2020 Presidential Election. *Misinformation Review*. https://misinforeview.hks.harvard.edu/article/research-note-examining-false-beliefs-about-voter-fraud-in-the-wake-of-the-2020-presidential-election/.

Spencer, Saranac Hale. (24 March 2021). Three False Claims about the Federal Voting Rights Bill. *FactCheck.org*. https://www.factcheck.org/2021/03/three-false-claims-about-the-federal-voting-rights-bill/.

## CHAPTER 12: POSTELECTION OBSTRUCTION: REFORMING PRESIDENTIAL TRANSITIONS

Beermann, Jack. (2006). The Constitutional Law of Presidential Transitions. *North Carolina Law Review*, 84.

Boston Consulting Group. (April 2020). *Presidential Transition Guide.* Center for Presidential Transition. https://presidentialtransition.org/wp-content/uploads/sites/6/2018/01/Presidential-Transition-Guide-2020.pdf.

Brauer, Carl M. (1989). *Presidential Transitions: Eisenhower through Reagan.* Oxford University Press.

Bur, Jessie. (10 December 2020). Will 2020 Election Change How Presidential Transitions Happen? *Federal Times.* https://www.federaltimes.com/management/2020/12/10/will-the-2020-election-change-how-presidential-transitions-happen/.

Hess, Stephen. (1 March 2001). First Impressions: A Look Back at Five Presidential Transitions. Brookings Institution. https://www.brookings.edu/articles/first-impressions-a-look-back-at-five-presidential-transitions/.

Hogue, Henry B. (13 November 2020). Presidential Transition Act: Provisions and Funding. *Congressional Research Service.* https://crsreports.congress.gov/product/pdf/R/R46602.

Seligman, Laura, and Bryan Bender. (20 January 2021). "Really Quite Shocking": Inside the Ugly Transition at the Pentagon. *Politico.* https://money.yahoo.com/really-quite-shocking-inside-ugly-180054170.html.

United States House of Representatives, House Committee on Oversight and Government Reform. (10 December 2020). *Hearing, The Elements of Presidential Transitions.* https://oversight.house.gov/legislation/hearings/the-elements-of-presidential-transitions.

Zoffer, Joshua B. (2020). The Law of Presidential Transitions. *Yale Law Journal*, 129.

## CHAPTER 13: RIGGED IF I LOSE, FAIR IF I WIN: PROTECTING ELECTION RESULTS

Bomboy, Scott. (15 December 2020). Explaining How Congress Settles Electoral College Disputes. *Constitution Daily.* https://constitutioncenter.org/blog/explaining-how-congress-settles-electoral-college-disputes.

Curtis, Charles, and Mark Medish. (7 October 2020). Navigating a Contested Election, the Electoral Vote Count Act and the 12th Amendment: How to Ensure a Fully Counted Outcome. *Just Security.* https://www.just

security.org/72700/navigating-a-contested-election-the-electoral-count-act
-and-12th-amendment-how-to-ensure-a-fully-counted-outcome/.

Editorial Board. (26 January 2021). The Law That Fueled the Capitol Riot. *Wall Street Journal.* https://www.wsj.com/articles/the-law-that-fueled-the -capitol-riot-11611704072.

Foley, Edward. (2016). *Ballot Battles: The History of Disputed Elections in the United States.* Oxford University Press.

Kilgore, Ed. (14 December 2020). Electoral College Rejects Trump Coup and Confirms Biden as President. *The Intelligencer.* https://nymag.com/intelli gencer/2020/12/electors-are-meeting-today-to-ratify-bidens-win.html.

Rybicki, Elizabeth, and L. Paige Whitaker. (8 December 2020). Counting Electoral Votes: An Overview of Procedures at the Joint Session, Including Objections by Members of Congress. *Congressional Research Service.* https:// fas.org/sgp/crs/misc/RL32717.pdf.

Schlicker, Eric, Terri L. Bimes, and Robert W. Mickey. (2001). *Safe at Any Speed: Legislative Intent, the Electoral Count Act of 1887, And BUSH v. GORE, Working Paper 2001-12.* Institute of Governmental Studies, University of California, Berkley. https://escholarship.org/uc/item/2q38565q

Siegel, Stephen A. (2004). The Conscientious Congressman's Guide to the Electoral Count Act of 1887. *Florida Law Review,* 56.

UChicago News. (8 January 2021). *Michael Albertus on the Lasting Impact of Trump's Attempts to Challenge the 2020 Election Results.* Political Science, University of Chicago. https://political-science.uchicago.edu/news/uchicago -news-michael-albertus-lasting-impact-trump%E2%80%99s-attempts -challenge-2020-election-results.

## CONCLUSION: PROMOTING CIVIC VIRTUE AND HEALING A DIVIDED AMERICA

Bauer, Bob, and Jack Goldsmith. (2020). *After Trump: Reconstructing the Presidency.* Lawfare.

Bessette, Joseph M., and John L. Pitney Jr. (2013). *American Government and Politics: Deliberation, Democracy and Citizenship.* Cengage.

Commission on the Practice of Democratic Citizenship. (2020). Our Common Purpose: Reinventing American Democracy for the 21st Century. *American Academy of Arts & Sciences.* https://www.amacad.org/sites/default/ files/publication/downloads/2020-Democratic-Citizenship_Our-Common -Purpose_0.pdf.

Educating for American Democracy Initiative. (2 March 2021). *Educating for American Democracy Report.* https://www.educatingforamericandemocracy

.org/wp-content/uploads/2021/02/Educating-for-American-Democracy
-Report-Excellence-in-History-and-Civics-for-All-Learners.pdf.

Ellmers, Glenn. (March 2021). "Conservatism" Is No Longer Enough. *American Mind.* https://americanmind.org/salvo/why-the-claremont-institute-is
-not-conservative-and-you-shouldnt-be-either/.

Lichtman, Allan J. (2008). *White Protestant America: The Rise of the American Conservative Movement.* Grove/Atlantic.

Orenstein, Jeffrey R. (2020). *Saving American Democracy: How We the People Can Be Truly Represented in Our Own Government.* Suncoast.

The President's Advisory 1776 Commission. (January 2021). *The 1776 Report.* https://ipfs.io/ipfs/QmVzW5NfySnfTk7ucdEoWXshkNUXn3dse
BA7ZVrQMBfZey.

# Index

# About the Author

Allan J. Lichtman is distinguished professor of history at American University and the author of many acclaimed books on U.S. political history, including *White Protestant Nation: The Rise of the American Conservative Movement*, which was a finalist for the National Book Critics Circle Award, *FDR and the Jews* (with Richard Breitman), and *The Case for Impeachment.* He is regularly sought out by the media for his authoritative views on voting and elections. He lives in Bethesda, Maryland.